Greenhorns in the Southwest

Calvin Rutstrum

GREENHORNS IN THE SOUTHWEST

Photographs by the Author

UNIVERSITY OF NEW MEXICO PRESS
Albuquerque

Library of Congress Cataloging in Publication Data
Rutstrum, Calvin.
    Greenhorns in the Southwest.

    1. New Mexico—Description and travel—1951–
2. Southwest, New—Description and travel—1951–
3. Rutstrum, Calvin.   4. Pecos Valley—Biography.
I. Title.
[F801.2.R8   1979]   917.89′04′5   79-4936
ISBN 0-8263-0512-1

©1972 by Calvin Rutstrum. All rights reserved. University of New Mexico Press paperback edition reprinted 1979 by arrangement with the author. Manufactured in the United States of America. Library of Congress Catalog Card Number 79-4936. International Standard Book Number 0-8263-0512-1.

Contents

Chapter One
Migration Southwest 11

Chapter Two
New Mexicana 23

Chapter Three
Adobe Abode 45

Chapter Four
"You Are What You Eat" 55

Chapter Five
A Day at Home in the Southwest 65

Chapter Six
On Poking Around 75

Chapter Seven
"Ranchero" 87

Chapter Eight
The Inscrutable Desert 103

Chapter Nine
New Mexican Wilderness Culture 117

Chapter Ten
  Anglophobia 133
Chapter Eleven
  Water 141
Chapter Twelve
  The Retirement Complex 151
Chapter Thirteen
  A Few Flies in the Ointment 161
Chapter Fourteen
  The More Natural Approach 171

Dedication

To my wife, Florence, who had less thorns under her saddle than I did.

A Sneak Preview of What It's About

As the title, *Greenhorns in the Southwest,* will suggest, the ensuing chapters are impressions of those who come upon a region strange to them, though fairly well equipped with an urban and natural background of living sufficient to make at least a common judgment. Consequently, there has been no designed effort herein to "gild the lily," rather I have tried to view the prospect as my wife and I found it, subjectively. Civic pride prefers all newcomers as well as deeply rooted citizens whenever they write about a region to "pretty up the landscape and turn on all neon lights." Few, however, are deceived by the allure of such pretentious nonsense, either in the scene proper or in the written word about a region. The Southwest needs no environmental apology; neither does it come off immaculately conceived by nature. Conventionally it has about the same ups and downs as the rest of the country, though I was pleasantly awed when in Silver City, New Mexico, I saw every car stop dead still at marked and unmarked intersections to allow pedestrians complete right-of-way, while in so many towns in the country, life continues in the street only by the athletic and agile dodge. I submit with arrogant egocentricity that the millions of tourists who head their cars into the Southwest, and those who plan to make permanent residency there, read this book before or on arrival. I think it will help to understand the Southwest as a true friend rather than as a casual acquaintance.

C. R.

Acknowledgments

The author wishes to thank:

Warren D. Yell of Las Cruces, New Mexico, for the photo illustration of the yucca in bloom.

Jack Drake of Carlsbad, New Mexico, for the photo illustration of his roadrunner wood carving.

The New Mexico Department of Development at Santa Fe, New Mexico, for the photo illustration of the ocotillo and the *horno* or *adobe* baking oven.

Chapter One

Migration Southwest

Ardent persuaders had sought to make the Southwest United States a tantalizing lure for me. For years I had managed to reject it. Annually on my wife's return from the Southwest she had given me a briefing on the fascination of the desert, until finally I compromised by agreeing to visit the region with her, provided she would permit me in our travels to put the strongest emphasis on its mountains.

The nature and fascination of mountains I could contemplate from experience, but the desert I was sure could have no particular appeal. I had been accustomed to canoe rivers that ran through magnificent coniferous forests, tundra rivers that widened into vast lake expanses or narrowed to tumble at intervals through canyons of thundering whitewater.

In winter, rather than head south, I sought snow and ice trails for dog sled or snowmobile treks through the same areas. My wife had followed me into the Far Northern regions so often, it seemed only fair that I should do her bidding on the Southwest at least once and join her seasonal migration. When she reminded me that I had been fascinated by canoe and dog sled travel across the tundra of the North, and that comparably the desert could be no less intriguing, the logic of my opposition sagged. We compromised by waiting until mid-January to leave the North.

The day we started out the temperature stood at 22 degrees below zero Fahrenheit in Minnesota. A fairly heavy accumulation of snow lay on the ground. It was unbelievable that within two to three days I could traverse enough latitude by car to leave sub-zero weather and the several feet of accumulated snow behind, and enter a near-summer climate. To

I had been accustomed to canoe rivers.

accomplish this in two or three days seemed phenomenal enough at the time, but later when this seasonal transition occurred in two or three hours by jet plane, I lost all sense of the geographical climate notions I had nurtured throughout life as a Northern resident.

The Far North that I knew had not yet been quite so striated with superhighways as the regions farther south where the roads paradoxically had a restriction against going too slow rather than too fast. As we drove southward, I gradually became aware of the change effected by latitude—the growth, the wildlife, the people and their varying cultures. One sensibly might stop often enough to observe, to contemplate—even to meditate a little on the wonders of latitudinal change effected by the sun's declination. Instead, I found myself on the kind of highways that excluded by regulatory decree just about every interest except one—DESTINATION.

I was reminded of the blinders put on horses years ago, which gave them a view of the road ahead and little else, lest they get diversionary notions or become spooked by scary side effects along the road.

One could now travel efficiently from coast to coast without gaining any truly significant knowledge of what lay along the route—trapped in a fissure of compelling ignorance from which no escape could be made until the director of highways gave his regimented permission to leave by the sign, "EXIT." These exits while permitting such periodical escape, too often proved to be routes to places of little or no interest, to deteriorating towns with poor or no service—lost enterprise, the will to live fading as the result of the highway bypass.

From our highway-imprisoned position, we pulled off on a shoulder at one point to examine with field glasses an attractive segment of near-distant country inaccessible from the highway. Before I had scarcely focused my view, a highway patrol car pulled up, and I was given a rather emphatic reprove for my "bad judgment" in stopping, even though I was off on a shoulder at least four feet from the edge of the blacktop. I apologized for breaking the rules of regimentation, and when I politely suggested that one could drive purblindly over the entire country without seeing anything worthwhile, or varying one's travel from the stereotyped, mathematically-spaced fuel and food stations, I was told by my highway disciplinarian that I had but a few seconds to get going into the blacktop groove or suffer the consequences of my violation. How intensely he enjoyed his moment of imperiousness!

I had my wife study the road map as we sped along, to see if it was not possible at some authorized exit to get off the superhighway and still proceed in a general southwesterly direction. Once we had made the escape through a legal exit, we found a blacktop, secondary road which veered off about five miles from and parallel to the superhighway.

Immediately, I felt a comfortable, luxurious freedom. The monolithic blinds were off. I could now vary my speed to fit mood and panorama, or capriciously pull off the road to meet the variable, numerous, beckoning interests along the way. It felt good not to be herded, or bullied

We noticed that in some of the Missouri road-cuts large masses of rock were agatized. Farmhouses, seemingly imperishable by time or weather, had been built out of this bedrock. A native resident who allowed us to inspect his home, told us that some of these houses were built during the early history of our nation. They were, we thought, like many of the people we met who lived in them—traditionally sound.

Now from time to time we were able to pull well off the road onto the turf or onto a side road to examine and identify the vegetation native to the region. With field glasses we were able to study the winter resident birdlife at different latitudes in wild ravine and upland. Every degree of latitude manifested observable change.

We talked to people about life in general whenever we could encounter them, around filling stations, at work mending fences, in farm ranch yards, in quiet villages, and where our high-clearance vehicle would go in out-of-the-way places. We were able to learn something of the daily life, the culture, history and traditions of various peoples and their backgrounds. Fascinating stories of early Missouri River history came from the descendants of those who lived along its banks, as though the eclipsed generations still had a voice. Not only were the people we visited apparently pleased by our interest, but they were equally generous with their information and hospitality—often abandoning the task of the moment to serve us coffee and to visit with us. They were proud, as certainly they should be, of their lineal history-making pioneer ancestry. It was not difficult during such visits to conjure up the precursors of the present residents fording the Missouri in Conestoga wagons to take up life at these very places.

The secondary blacktop road on which we traveled continued favorably some distance south, but in order that we might travel west to gain on the southwesterly direction, we sought a turn. At the first such turn was a small coffee shop with a single residence nearby. It seemed another inviting place to pause. Within were three substantial wooden tables with four ruggedly-built, comfortable, wooden chairs at each table. The place had a clean, farm-kitchen coziness and freshness about it. We were cordially greeted by a young couple as we entered, but they made no overtures to wait on us. Finally, I asked: "Could we have some coffee, please?"

"Yes, surely," said the young lady member of the couple. "We just thought you wanted to *set* a spell."

"Well, yes," I thought, happily, "but could one have guessed that people still existed who had such commendable leisure in a restless, petulant world?"

Here was no imposing commercialism, no nerve-wracking tension, no subtly hidden suggestion that you bolt your food and get under way to make room for others heading down a regimented highway. We were served with the warmth and courtesy of people who enjoyed people and leisure.

I thought about the strait-laced, stereotyped fuel and food stations on the superhighway. They were modern, clean, plastic-veneered, efficiently run. But every waitress said about the same thing, moved in about the same methodically propelled manner, as though wholly destitute of her own individual, sincere courtesy. I pictured them uniformly lined up at attention in their training classes—warm, beautiful human beings converted to stereotyped robots.

This is probably an "efficient" way to run such a chain of restaurants. But as I left the little byway coffee shop I did not find myself stridently roaring off to reach the minimum superhighway speed and driving headlong to another mathematically-spaced fuel and food station, ditto, ditto impulsively to destination. I carried away the richness and warmth of fine association, a feeling of earlier travel when you might "Take thine ease at mine inn."

I was once told that an experiment had been made in a laboratory of putting a frog in a basin of cold water, then gradually heating the water to see at what exact temperature the frog would jump out. It didn't jump; it cooked to death. The change from North to South was that gradual, but not at all tragic. When I left the North at 22 degrees below zero and its several feet of snow, I was anxious to note where the first open ground would appear. As the miles slipped by, the change was so imperceptible, I forgot that deep snow cover had been a substantial part of the early route.

Without noting where the transition from snow cover to open ground had been, I became aware that cattle were grazing on dry range grass. Vegetation species unfamiliar in my Northern life began to appear. Yucca suddenly grew along the route. I pulled off the road to examine what I thought was an especially fine specimen.

Such growth as sacaton grass was registering on my mind for the first time.

I had previously been crash-reading about Southwest flora and fauna in order to take a first knowledgeable step on Southwest ground. Quite familiar with much plant and animal life in the North, here in this land I became the raw initiate. Such growth as the yucca, agave, bear and sacaton grasses, except from text, were registering for the first time on my mind as real live images.

I had read about the yucca root having penetrated the ground even to a depth of 40 feet in the White Sands region of New Mexico in its surviving probe for moisture. Its fibers, I learned, have been used by the Indians for making baskets, rope, mats, sandals, even coarse cloth; its fruit and seeds used for food and drink; its saponifying roots for soap uses, especially for shampoo, having a quality for beautifying the hair. (Cosmeticians, please take note!) I was surprised to read that only the *Pronuba*

I had read about the yucca and its varied uses.

A species of yucca, sometimes called Spanish sword.

The austerity of the Southwest range.

"Forty acres to a mother cow."

moth can pollinate the yucca. Both yucca and *Pronuba* moth would die were it not for the age-old ecological marriage of these life companions.

A reference gave the following:

> (This strange moth, according to scientific data, belongs to the order *Tegeticula*. There are various species and each is adapted for pollinization to its own particular species of yucca. The moths developed from larva, emerge when the flower opens, and roll together balls of pollen which they carry to another flower. The moths then lay 4 to 5 eggs in the pistil and insert the pollen mass. The larva when hatched consumes 20 or so of about 200 seeds for food during their development, leaving about a hundred seeds to perpetuate the species.)

There seems to be a moral here in equity.

I had driven far enough off to the side of secondary roads to avoid risking arrest and penalty for observing the natural wonders of life and the social culture along the way. A highway patrolman, nevertheless, stopped to ask if I was in trouble. (People apparently never stop unless for gas, to eat, or when in trouble.) "Not really," I said, "but could you tell me something about this miracle plant?"

"I sure as hell can. They're a damn nuisance in this country. There ought to be some way of getting rid of them, but the job would cost more than the Fort Knox gold."

"But why get rid of them? Just think how wonderful the nature of this plant really is," I insisted. "It provided food, drink, and clothing as well as other benefits for the Indian. It has one of the strangest and most interesting pollinization characteristics for propagation. Only one insect in the world, the *Pronuba* moth, will keep it propagating."

He looked at me with an expression something akin to pity, and said:

"You're welcome to all you want."

I was sort of happy to learn that the yucca after all had won the battle against threatened extinction by human predation.

The highway patrolman did, however, ask what a *Pronuba* moth was, which I thought was somewhat encouraging.

Cattle ranged on both sides of the road and swarmed in mud-mired, though well kept, sophisticated feeding pens that smelled to high heaven, but it is not offensive to those of us who have ridden the range and handled stock.

Accustomed to dense, lush grass, knee-deep in the Northern summer, I was amazed at the austerity that prevailed on the Southwest range, where little tufts of various highly nourishing grama grasses and other widely spaced plants offered the chief sustaining forage for the scattered herds. A high percentage of not too astute cattlemen, I was told by agricultural experts, had so overgrazed the range, there was little chance for moisture to be retained in the soil to build up a substantial growth. Cattlemen who practiced wisdom in this respect, it was indicated, were in too small a proportion to bring about the much-needed control legislation. Therefore, winds reaching more than a comfortable velocity, lifted the dust from overgrazed ranges to darken the day and bring visibility to near zero.

Government range lands leased by ranchers, on the other hand, were controlled—the basis being so many acres, as high as 40 or more, to a mother cow. "Forty acres to a mother cow," the allocation seemed to have a sort of poetic austerity. The government range land lessees, I was advised, fought control, intent upon pursuing their illogical scorched earth grazing methods. Since dust storms that blow from overgrazed private land affect the lands of sensible ranchers as well, we have an obtrusive injustice, affecting all in town and country alike. To suggest government interference with such range methods would be to arouse the politicians of a noted breed who continually howl government interference with private enterprise.

CHAPTER TWO

New Mexicana

As we rolled into New Mexico on Highway 54, there was an increasing rough grandeur in the scenery—a refreshing relief from the flat prairie through which we had traveled. New Mexican terrain seemed to have the best identifiable demarkation for entry into what might truly be considered the Southwest. Great mesas (table lands) rose imposingly on all sides of the highway, interspersed with arroyos and alluring, rockbound gorges that caught the oblique red and orange light of the late afternoon sun with such magnificence as to send one into paroxysms of exclamation over the changing spectacle. In Texas a filling station attendant, learning that we were headed for New Mexico, said, "Oh, so you're going into the pretty country."

Charles F. Lummis, in describing New Mexico, wrote: ". . . nor is there elsewhere on the earth such an exposition of earth-carving forces as the unique Mesa Country . . . its table-topped islands in the air . . ."

The Spanish-Mexican-Indian mixture at once became predominant within the borders of New Mexico, as though one had just crossed an international boundary. My wife would now, she said, introduce me to the culinary delicacies of Mexican fare. She had been speaking of *sopaipillas,* a kind of deep-fat-fried, globular doughnut or puff, which for want of Spanish pronunciation, we more readily referred to as "sofa pillows." These were the bread complement to most Mexican meals. Then there was the *frijole,* the Mexican pinto bean that has been and still is a great mainstay for the Indians. The *frijole* intrigued me by its early history—a legume containing an amazingly high protein content and other valuable

Great mesas (tablelands) rose imposingly.

food constituents. I had been duly warned about the hot chili dishes, some so hot as to "burn the lint out of your navel."

Well into New Mexico we found a highly recommended Mexican cafe. Its walls were adorned with painted guitars, sombreros, pack burros, gay shawls, and whatever symbolically suggested Mexico in its most traditional and romantic state. The floor was covered with an inch-deep carpet of green-dyed sawdust.

I expected to see a black-haired, dark-eyed senorita approach us with a menu containing all of the strange, to us, entrees peculiar to Mexican cooking. Had she carried castanets in the other hand and given us a few clicking alerts, I would not have been surprised. Instead, a blue-eyed, ripe-wheatfield blonde waitress sauntered in, with a demeanor which suggested that her previous night's date had either been a dud, or proved to be something more than she had bargained for. I asked her about the various entrees and found them as foreign to her as they were to us.

"Aren't you Spanish?" I asked, suspecting the power of TV advertised hair bleach commercials.

"No," she said. "I'm a Swede from Kansas."

I settled on an order of *tacos* with a side dish of *frijoles,* but the *frijoles* which I had most wanted to try, somehow in the final serving of our dinner failed to show up. We compromised the situation by ordering a dessert, choosing at random from the intriguing items of the menu, *pastel de calabaza.* The term, I thought, would turn up something exotic. It turned out to be pumpkin pie.

At Santa Rosa, New Mexico, we entered a cafe owned by "Anglos" who specialize in pinto beans and chuck wagon sourdough biscuits. Both of these started a later dietary trend in our own domestic household. When later we purchased two take-out paper containers of cooked pinto beans, a Mexican-type bystander who apparently thought we were needlessly indulging in extravagance, said: "My God, man, don't you know how to cook pinto beans?" Evidently, no matter how you cook them, success is inevitable. If only all cooking could have such promising results.

Having a sort of geographical passion for maps and other documentary material, we bought whatever we could find on the Southwest. Studying this material, we saw the Southwest at a broad glance in a pattern of what appears to be four distinct, general areas: the Colorado Plateau covering the north-central portion, the Great Basin Desert over its south and west, the Great Plains occupying its eastern third or less, and the wide tongue of the Rocky Mountains, extending deep into the north central part and rising over 13,000 feet. From these mountains flow the historical Rio Grande, the Pecos, and the Colorado rivers, elbowing their way through the mountain valleys and foothills with a generous flow, much of the water becoming greatly attenuated along the way as irrigated tracts blot up the water supply through the desert.

Just as these rivers hold to a course redirected only by the effects of man's irrigation dams and by the gradual erosion meander, the tourist likewise, most often narrows his scope with little variation of travel within the New Mexican "canyon walls" of its highways. From what I

We took to the saddle horse and foot trails.

had learned by a more critical reading and inquiry, most of New Mexico's charm does not lie along its highways. We would have to leave the beaten path of the average tourist and travel the dirt road byways, the river valleys, the mountain passes, and box canyons, really to see the splendor of New Mexico. Consequently, we abandoned the "Carry-All" where it became doubtful transportation, and took to the jeep, the saddle and pack horse, and foot trails. Had we not pursued this diversified course, our impression of the Southwest would have been a completely misguided, prosaic tour.

I would make one fleeting trip to the Southwest, I had thought while back in the North. Now I was caught in the fascination of its inescapable wilderness attractions, its archaeological mysteries, its genial climate—and the list goes on.

Before leaving the town of Santa Rosa, I had gone to the banks of the Pecos River in the town to observe the general aspect of Southwest rivers. Sand bars hung out of water like great dry tongues parching in the sun. I was, for the moment, disappointed. I had been accustomed in the North to voluminous, rushing rivers. The Pecos' meager flow ran lazily around the protruding sand bars. Local and perfunctory observations, however, can be deceptive. I speculated on what the country might possibly be along the north and south banks away from the town. These questions I bandied about until I got some fairly lucrative answers from long-time Santa Rosa citizens.

An active head of civic affairs in town said, "If you want to see some really unusual scenery, take a ten-mile drive south of town along the Pecos to the end of the narrow blacktop." At the time of my visit with him I stood on a street corner where I could observe the country quite advantageously for nearly a mile to the south along the river. It looked flat and uninspiring. I suspected, therefore, that I had been talking to one with more civic pride than an appreciation or recognition of natural beauty. Yet, until I knew more about the river, the best part of valor, I felt, was to assume a sympathetic response and a yet-to-be qualified optimism. He did not particularize on what the "unusual scenery" would be. Were it not for my normal, insatiable curiosity, I might have wholly disregarded his suggestion to head down river.

The next morning I told my wife with a chuckle that we were supposed to explore the Pecos south of town for unusual scenery. She looked at me, then at the uninterrupted staked plains, smiled but said nothing. In her silence I sensed a rather well-qualified skepticism.

The road, a narrow but good quality meandering blacktop, crossed a deep, refreshing trout stream at the edge of town—the El Rito—though the view beyond it gave no indication that we were to cross anything more than a continuing flat, or at most a gentle rolling plain. About a mile out of town the road veered to the left, then gained a rather substantial rise. The flat, grassy plain merged as we drove on, into a rough outcropping of bedrock, where the selection of a roadbed had been restricted to a single choice of contour. Here the road swung off to the left, mounted a rocky ridge, and rose as it seemed for a moment, "into the sky."

The road mounted a rocky ridge—and rose, as it seemed, "into the sky."

I had heard the stock expressions of amazement on coming upon the Grand Canyon for the first time, "Golly, what a gully!" and others, but perhaps the most salutary reaction as we suddenly came over the rise and looked down into the grand Pecos canyon was our awe-inspired silence. We pulled to the roadside and stared. A sudden transition from a rolling plain to a spectacular winding gorge, the river now flowed with a generous volume of water around imposing bluff and mesa. It was all incredibly surprising.

Where did the sudden flow of water come from?

We investigated. The famous Blue Hole, and ten small "bottomless," spring-fed lakes in the vicinity of Santa Rosa were apparently responsible for swelling the Pecos stream, now flashing like a broad silver ribbon in the eternal New Mexican sun. Federal and State fish hatcheries had been established on opposite sides of the river as a result of this water supply.

We swung on down into the canyon over the winding, narrow blacktop, the canyon walls towering above us. The road closely skirted the river here and there wherever the escarpments and talus slopes crowded the river channel. Flocks of wildfowl rose and beat a rapid retreat down the valley, returning to pass high above us again and again. I remarked that this was January when three to five feet of ice covered the lakes and rivers of the summer nesting grounds of wildfowl in Canada. It was difficult for me, a Northerner, to equate running water and flocks of wildfowl with midwinter.

Even a scant half-dozen degrees of latitude south of snowbound Minnesota, we had seen en route into the Southwest, great flocks of geese languishing in open water. The effect upon a Northerner is a sort of seasonal transition—a kind of pseudo-spring—that upsets the annual chronology long sustained within one's nature by habit. It is comparable to driving a dog sled in the sub-zero Yukon and coming upon hot springs where green vegetation flourishes, which actually happens on the Nahanni River in northwest Canada.

Ten miles from Santa Rosa, New Mexico, we reached the sleepy-looking *adobe* village of Puerto de Luna (Portal to the Moon)—a village trembling on the verge of indecision as to whether it shall become a ghost town or, when activated, spring into a prospering community. The latter, judging by the geographical nature of its setting, seems to be most likely in the offing.

We talk amusingly, and at times regretfully, about ghost towns in the Southwest—their early life from inception to demise—but scarcely ever do we speculate on their resurrection. The death of a town, apparently, leaves far greater potentials, however, than mere "ghosts." The government recently, we learned, has even seen fit to restore ghost-town buildings of historical significance, simulating their early images, or if remaining, they need only be steadied structurally on their foundations to stand upright again and dignified as monuments in the life of the Southwest.

We had seen great flocks of geese languishing in open water.

Puerto de Luna, a village trembling on the verge of indecision.

We came to discover that nostalgia for the old develops factions continually battling with factions who seek to demolish the old for the new. One, of course, sees this conflict everywhere in the world. Priceless architectural landmarks stand precariously on sites of great real estate value. Or, as in the ghost town, the tax dollar cannot readily be allocated to save historical monuments. The tax dollar is needed in too many places, and allied to this incontestable fact is the lack of understanding the more profound human values when it comes to spending that tax dollar.

One gains a feeling of national pride when government steps in to bolster culture in any respect, its much-neglected role. Political concern has largely been slanted toward saving material equities—too little emphasis it seems on the song of life. Emphasis on industry to supply the physical needs of man will lose no consideration, we can be sure, in a pragmatic world. It is time, I think, to note the art design on the useful pot, for it is the design that most ennobles life, even though the pot itself must materially sustain it.

But culture, it became evident to us, no matter how sublime, is not alone apt to raise a ghost town. Man must fill his stomach before he can contemplate and praise the sunset. VISTA (Volunteers in Service to America) now working hand in hand with townspeople may be the adrenaline hypo which will arouse ghost towns from their semiconsciousness. If cooperative markets and crafts started by VISTA could be maintained by sufficient patronage, it could bring the reviving breath of life to many slumbering ghost towns.

The coming-to-life of a ghost town must inevitably set up a chain of reflective thought in which the question arises: "Why did the original town emerge from the desert soil in the first place, continue through perhaps a century of activity and then suffer such retrogression that all human activity stopped? And why did it so lie dormant for a number of silent decades, then finally emerge as vibrantly alive again as though the dormant interval had not existed?" A probe in depth might reveal the true facts about this dilemma, but the transitions as they occurred seem historically more dramatic, more romantic if we do not examine them too critically.

We stopped at an old abandoned store building in Puerto de Luna, where we were told that *Billy the Kid* had periodically bought supplies—

A store building where *Billy The Kid* had bought supplies.

the storekeeper and his family fleeing whenever The Kid's horses were seen approaching through the Pecos Canyon. The integrity of The Kid was said to have been the best when he dealt with the natives. He would help himself to supplies from their store shelves and leave money in payment for them lying on the counter. It was from such fragments of The Kid's behavior that a strange, sympathetic legend has been built up around him.

His story, many insist, carried a strong conviction of extenuating circumstances, in which he was provoked into a commendably defensive position. Others think that his biographers have built a fascinating though largely fictional legend on a foundation of inexcusable, reckless misconduct and murder. Apparently he is revered, or the novelty of his adventurous life intrigues, for his grave at Fort Sumner, New Mexico, is visited

The grave of *Billy The Kid*, chipped by tourists.

by thousands of tourists who chipped away at his tombstone for souvenirs until a heavy grill had to be built around it for protection.

Bandit or ravaging conquistador, adulation for them is an eternal condonement. Coronado came to the Southwest to repeat what had been perpetrated on the Inca civilization. He heard about the Seven Cities of Cibola in New Mexico, inhabited by wealthy tribes of Indians whose villages were believed to be clad in gold. The criminal presumptuousness that he had the prerogative to mass murder these Indians if necessary and plunder their wealth to have possession has been popularly accepted as an act of equitable exploration propriety. Though a scoundrel and a thief in his motive, we found him lauded everywhere. He appears in every textbook as an exalted "Conquistador," a sad commentary, we have to say, on the general standard of ethics and certainly a despicable perversion by historical writers on the Southwest who make laudable his heinous actions. (It is a strange quirk in mankind that man chooses to celebrate criminals. Efforts to build statues for Jesse James, Soapy Smith, and other such infamous characters, have constantly to be discouraged by the better thinking citizenry.)

The Seven Cities of Cibola gold myth apparently originated from the sight of cliffs covered with a yellow-colored lichen, giving a gold sheen in the sun to this symbiotic white and yellow growth on the rocks.

Coronado's committed guide who suffered the Seven Cities of Cibola gold illusion, was threatened with death if he did not properly guide Coronado's heavily armed, military band of thieves to the object of their murder and plunder. The Coronado march ended in disaster somewhere in Kansas, with great suffering, thirst, and starvation in its ranks, caused by its obvious heavy-handedness and wilderness incompetence. On the basis of the band's motives, one might have hoped that the consequences had been even more excruciatingly painful to Coronado and his band, more wrought with bitter disappointment, more agonizing death and frustration. The thought of Coronado's return, shamefaced, to report to his criminally avaricious crowned heads, his utter failure to ravage another culture is a thought that refreshes. One lives sympathetically with every Apache who stalked Coronado's band at each water hole, leaving them dry-tongued, hopeless, dying from thirst, hunger, and despair. What a grand chapter it would have been in history to celebrate, if the Incas had imposed such a cunning strategy of terrifying retaliation, or worse, on their invaders.

Somehow, Puerto de Luna, New Mexico, became the first focal point in our intimate association with the Southwest, its history, land and people. Little did we realize then that its focus was to become more critical as we left it and started the trek through the Southwest. As conquistadors ourselves, though with less reprehensible motives, we had already planned to conquer the Southwest, but only by assimilation of its priceless values, I assure you, arrogating to ourselves as much knowledge of New Mexico's wilderness culture as possible. We decided to go even farther than that as our interest grew, as knowledge was gained, and as the people of the Southwest became more fascinating with every contact.

We decided to buy some land.

But where?

There was Phoenix, Arizona, on which such a vast population had converged, and Tucson—both with real estate booms so loud they could be heard round the world. There was Albuquerque and Santa Fe and inescapable Taos, once you were at Santa Fe. These cities were considered only radially. Where, we speculated, in the outward radius of one of them would we consider property? Phoenix was the first to be scratched from our agenda. Then Tucson, and finally the whole state of Arizona. Next, we had to scratch Albuquerque, Santa Fe and Taos because they were in altitudes that made winter residence not sufficiently different from the North, though, of course, considerably milder in temperature. The perimeter of Phoenix was scratched to avoid being trampled underfoot by the converging population increase; Tucson as well. One region, Oak Creek Canyon in Arizona, had its indigenous clutches so deep within us, a light breeze in the right direction might have toppled our sentiments in favor of settling there. Its magnificence and diversified interest have been told in so many ways, a further description would be extravagant redundancy. But thousands of people believed as we believed—and what Oak Creek Canyon was and what it soon will be is the difference between willful thinking and grim reality. If, as I have stated elsewhere, and risk repeating, "Thousands come here seeking solitude," it best describes what we would face by settling in Oak Creek Canyon, where nature in sheer grandeur has outdone herself.

I suppose that we felt very much like the people in the early covered-wagon treks across the land. Many of them never got to California because they were fascinated by intervening land areas. Arizona undiscovered, one has to insist, was some kind of miraculous creation. Fifty years ago I would not have escaped its attractions, a statement that also applies to California. We were not exactly sloughed off from the main covered-wagon caravan headed for a promised land. We simply came back to New Mexico, getting in, as it were, out of the rain of preconceived illusions.

I often humorously answer people who live in Southern California when they ask why I did not settle there, that I intended to but got on one of those superhighways and wasn't able to get off until I reached New Mexico.

The specifications I laid down to real estate brokers screened out all land development schemes. The acreage, I insisted, would have to be fronting on water, perhaps on a mountain stream, where to gain the advantage of a mild temperature, the stream first reached the desert level. It did not necessarily have to be on a good auto road, just so that it was at least accessible by two ruts meandering through the wilderness over which I could reach the site with a four-wheel drive, high-clearance, jeep-like vehicle. If not that, I would in the extreme settle for access by saddle and pack horse.

One of the real estate dealers whom I approached was somewhat amused when I laid down these specifications, especially the part about the water frontage. Himself a former resident of the Upper Midwest United States, his immediate response was:

"I know just the place for you."

"Where?"

"Northern Wisconsin."

Despite the agent's apparent pessimism, the Gila Wilderness area in the southwestern part of New Mexico did appear to have outstanding possibilities in meeting the specifications, but I was already entranced by the grandeur of the Pecos Canyon below Santa Rosa. Nevertheless, I cautiously ranged far and wide by whatever adaptable means of travel a further search for the ultimate in a cabin site required. One thing seemed apparent, the search would now be confined to the less populated New Mexico.

Among the beautiful, white-splotched trunks and spreading limbs of the sycamores on the Gila there was an excellent tract fronting on a fascinating part of the river with a good volume of water soon after the stream had left the higher altitudes of the mountains. Unfortunately, the canyon walls here are so high, I found, as to shut out sunlight for all but the midday hours.

Once back in the Santa Rosa area, I had considered throwing myself at the mercy of real estate agents again for a possible tract on the Pecos but for a fortunate coincidence that took place while indulging in a late cup of coffee just before closing time in a Santa Rosa cafe. Being the only remaining customer at this late hour, I remarked to the waitress during our conversation that I was interested in the purchase of a possible tract on the Pecos.

And just as casually she remarked, "Maybe I'll sell you our place."

The property, as she described it, consisted of ten acres, five under irrigation, and a three-room *adobe* cabin fronting on the river a mile downstream from the tiny village of Puerto de Luna, accessible by a maintained dirt road from the blacktop, and served with electric power. A telephone line was being considered. I could scarcely wait until morning to examine the property.

The Pecos Canyon on this second trip seemed even more exciting and awe-inspiring the next morning, now that it might turn out to be a route to one's own residence. This may be egocentricity, sentimentality, or whatever one wishes to call it; but it's a good feeling. On the dirt road leading from the blacktop to the site, we passed a mule cart, which was courteously turned off the road by its aged driver, to let us pass. The driver had been up in the hills for a load of piñon-pine stove wood. We caught the piney fragrance of the freshly cut wood as it passed. Were it not for a pickup truck equipped with a cattle rack parked in the village, we might well have identified the settlement, the mule cart and all, with life centuries ago. All of the buildings here had been made of *adobe* or native stone bonded with *adobe* mortar.

The view stretched a mile or more across the palisaded Pecos Valley.

Behind the *adobe* cabin rose a two-mile-long mesa.

The ditch had more the semblance of a mountain stream.

In view from our patio, we saw the Pecos—full-flowing.

As we neared the property, our interest rose. From the doorway of the *adobe* cabin I found that the view stretched a mile or more across the palisaded Pecos Valley to the west, where the setting sun would drop behind the canyon wall as behind a mountain. Several miles toward the south, and about as many to the north, the river flashed its sensuous curves in the high-riding New Mexican sun. Behind the *adobe* cabin rose a two-mile-long mesa that formed the west wall of what we were later to learn was an interest-packed, picturesque, spring-fed box canyon.

Water, the most sought-after element in any desert country, seemed here at the property site almost in excess. Under the concrete patio we found a three-thousand-gallon cistern filled to the brim from the season's rains. About forty feet from the cabin door we observed an irrigation ditch flowing around enormous cottonwood trees—the ditch suggesting by its two centuries of assimilation to the region as having more the semblance of a mountain stream than a canal excavation by man. Several hundred feet below the irrigation ditch in full view from our patio, we saw the Pecos River—full-flowing, fed from the lakes and the Blue Hole previously mentioned.

Mapwise, according to its cartographers, we were in the Chihuahuan Desert, an area designated as *arid*. Yet, we had more water sources than might be found in the average nonarid region. In fact, we learned that the community was also contemplating a domestic water project, supplied from a generous canyon spring area, and that a pipeline had already been staked out along the dirt road that served our property—thus providing even a possible fourth source of water.

At this point I would have enjoyed a little humorous banter with the earlier patronized real estate agent who had suggested that I was geographically on a doubtful search for waterfront property in the desert.

The situation was, of course, unusual—the property a valuable discovery—and we bought it. Here we have the paradoxical situation of being in a wilderness area with a facility for all improvements, together with other natural advantages. We might have settled for much less—and I reflected on the turn of events that a late cup of coffee could determine in the course of one's life.

Giant cottonwoods belied the remotest suggestion of desert.

Two mule deer regularly grazed on our irrigated alfalfa field. Along the river, beaver cuttings—some old, some fresh—were scattered along the banks. The numerous giant cottonwood trees along the river and along the irrigation ditch belied the remotest suggestion of a desert. Hugging the mesas behind the cabin, incredibly spaced by nature, were countless juniper and piñon pine trees. Peach, delicious-type apples, plum, apricot and cherry trees stood neatly spaced in a small orchard. Desert? The appellation seemed so inappropriate.

The irrigation, after serving us, serves another small ranch below and then rejoins the waters of the Pecos. From here on for twenty miles, there is no irrigation, the river winding its way through a wild canyon that features the true elements of natural, inviolate New Mexico. On river shelves we found the remains of ancient Indian campgrounds, the

On river shelves we found the remains of stone shelters.

We found such artifacts as arrowheads, flint knives, etc.

Metates—some as perfect as though in use yesterday.

It is the intriguing Chihuahuan Desert that holds most of our interest.

stone shelters fallen into rubble. In the immediate area of these ruins, we found such artifacts as arrowheads, flint knives, pottery, metates (mill stones) and monos, some as perfect as though made or used yesterday.

In the North I had foresworn any affinity for the desert. Now I had succumbed to its particular charms.

The Sangre de Cristos, a range of the Rocky Mountains, rise a short drive from our cabin, and while we go to them for an occasional packhorse trip late in the spring, it is the intriguing Chihuahuan Desert that holds most of our attention during the months we spend annually in the Southwest.

CHAPTER THREE

Adobe Abode

A severe art critic once said, "If you can draw a perfectly straight line free-handed, you are a draftsman, not an artist." By the same token in building an *adobe* house, if one too diligently applies level and square, there cannot result that charm which is essentially *adobe*. Formal symmetry, somehow, does not lend itself effectively to the free-hand, sensuous curves of *adobe* structures.

We have, perhaps, a comparable example of overly symmetrical construction where a firm now creates perfectly-formed, lathe-turned logs for log cabin construction. From such symmetry the picturesque log cabin effect departs. Something artistically elusive somehow takes flight in the mathematically precise form. (Can it be because there is no perfectly straight line or perfect circle in nature?)

Dorothy L. Pillsbury, who writes so charmingly about *adobe,* titles an article of hers "A-D-O-B-E SPELLS CONTENTMENT." With this I think all who are familiar with *adobe* can agree. But most I fear would disagree with her that it is primarily ". . . the Anglo convert to *adobe* who has made of *adobe*-living a philosophy and a song."

Also, I think we have to disagree with the charming lady that to the cult of *adobe*-lovers, brickmaking, floor plans, *vigas, canales, portales, patios* and corner fireplaces, these are "all surface stuff." The essential notes of *adobe* are too intricately involved to subordinate them without losing the grand effect of the song.

I haven't fully concluded what constitutes a qualified member of the "cult," though I have met a few who seemed doctrinally and readily given over to *adobeist* tenets. Those *adobe* cultists whom I have cornered to celebrate the rites of their edifices were at once fascinated by a treatise on the elemental aspects of *adobe*. And I must confess that when I first learned about *adobe,* my curiosity was immediately aroused as to why a certain kind of mud could have the properties and qualities of determining to a marked degree the cultural evolution of mankind in a region wherever such soil was to be found.

The secret of the properties inherent in *adobe* is apparently bound up in the one word *caliche,* it being the calcium carbonate which forms the bonding element in certain soils. The physical and chemical properties of caliche could involve us in much scientific study. But what primarily interests the dweller of an *adobe* house and concerns him elementally are the physical aspects of the *adobe* material itself which combine to make the *adobe* house so habitable and charming. Fourteen to thirty-six-inch-thick *adobe* walls, varying from dwelling to public building, provide all-in-one structural strength, insulation, and other features which amaze the *adobe* initiate. The fact that modern mechanical improvements can be buried in *adobe* walls more readily than in any other kind of construction, is another abiding *adobe* facility in its modern-day favor. In fact, *adobe* walls so absorb these modern gadgets as to suggest to the non*adobe* dweller that the *adobe* house is not modern at all.

While the *adobe* at its best deviates attractively from the symmetrical, and very old *adobes* usually have been built by nontradesmen who were not as a rule too skilled in setting in window openings, it does not apply that door and window openings must remain drafty as they so often are. Being a sort of perfectionist by nature, I was a bit chary about occupying an *adobe* house with a reputation for poorly fitting openings. We are told, "Look once if you want to see beauty, look twice if you want to be critical." I have, no doubt, suffered long from the critical look, and consequently I have, perhaps, missed much of life's beauty. But to have the soft unsymmetrical lines of *adobe* and no drafts—that seemed an achievement. I thus had all of the unsquare window and door frames of our *adobe* taken out and replaced with heavy, perfectly aligned, cemented-in frames and heavy doors, ruggedly studded with wrought iron. Here, symmetry

The *adobe* cabin as we found it *before* remodeling and modernizing.

We tried to take the best of the original *adobe*—losing something, gaining something.

lost nothing. The doors now open and close as tightly as a safe, draft-free, though a severe dust storm still does manage a slight dust deposit just inside the door.

We need have no illusions about the evolutionary change in the *adobe* house. It has not been taken in toto—as some purists persist—from its earliest form. Like the American language, which used "the best of many languages," for most comprehensive expression and communication, we have tried to take the best of the original *adobe,* losing something, perhaps, but gaining something too.

Basically, *adobe* as a building material unquestionably has inherent structural advantages which in the complete edifice call for superlatives to describe its potentials for charming living—but there the *adobe* as an original entity ceases.

The original *adobe* rose from the ground and the forest in rather primitive form. The floor was of *adobe* dirt, hardened with ox blood to prevent the continual trituration by footsteps from keeping the air within fogged with dust. Walls went up as they do today with form-molded *adobe* mud bricks dried in the sun, of a size that could easily be handled by one man, and readily set in *adobe* mortar. The *vigas* we see today have become architecturally symbolic of *adobe,* and who would say they do not lend charm as they protrude from the *adobe* which is molded around them. But few *adobe* houses of today need—except as ornament—the *vigas* that seem so compatible, so in complement with the *adobe* itself. Originally, *vigas* were the small-diameter logs taken roughly from the forest to support the great weight of dirt that formed the roof. A heavy carpet of branches was laid on the *vigas,* then seal-plastered with *adobe* mud, a thick roof of dirt finally piled on to insulate from the cold, and to shed the rain and snow.

Numerous *adobe* houses today have mere log stubs inserted into the *adobe* to simulate the *viga* effect. The effect is very good, but it is a mere pretension. Generally the roof is constructed of plank rafters from the lumber yard, the roof commercially insulated, lumber sheathed, and a built-up asphalt weather-shedding roof surface applied, but no dirt. Occasionally, "store-bought" insulated roofs do have dirt added, but this also is a pretension to simulate the ancient *adobe.*

The *adobe* cultists need have no frustrations, however, in knowing these facts, for after all, it is the actual element of *adobe* which surrounds them with charm, warmth of feeling, and which inspires "a philosophy and a song."

The *fogón,* that unique, molded, beehive-like corner fireplace, the flaming jewel in the *adobe* house, never fails to focus attention. In the corner it is a structural and artistic "natural," structurally because it becomes greatly simplified, the corner walls of the *adobe* house contributing much of its entire form. It needs little more than the addition of an *adobe* front facet from floor to ceiling and a chimney above the roof to complete it, though the inner construction is a bit tricky. It needs a back draft shelf to keep it from smoking into the room.

Any play of fancy should, of course, be condoned, and when the *fogón* suggests to some that it becomes the campfire moved indoors by the very nature of its design, the thought is not farfetched. The narrowness of the corner *fogón,* where the wood is set on end, or pyramided, is believed so constructed to simulate this campfire concept. But the Indian style of campfire for heat and cooking outdoors was scarcely ever the vertically-fed or tepee-arranged fire. Structural factors in the corner *fogón* seem to rest largely on two impelling principles—the facility it provides for supporting the opening, needing no steel lintel across the top of the opening, so necessary in modern, wide-opening fireplaces, and because the small rooms in the earlier *adobe* dwellings needed but a small wood-conserving fire. Early tools for bucking up firewood having been much less efficient than what we now use, must also have influenced the fire-size though wood was no doubt more plentiful. Setting the fireplace in a corner also becomes an advantage because of the ninety-degree view angle it provides.

We can presume that the integral or blending aspect of the *adobe fogón* with the *adobe* structure itself, has much to do with its charm. I suppose that the true phrase is *in complement.* One need only encompass native piñon pine fragrantly burning in the *fogón* of an *adobe* dwelling, decked with scarlet *ristras* of chili peppers, adding the other intimate, immediate native accoutrements that make up life in the Southwest home, to discover that more natural parts fall into place here in life's mosaic than a greenhorn from the North might ever expect to discover when first he unloads his "covered wagon" for settlement.

This blending of natural elements seems almost overwhelming in prospect when we first learn that walls of *adobe* are merely the horizontal earth turned up ninety degrees. How can an *adobe* thus fail to blend with the environment? I am not prone to carry this idea of earthiness to the point suggested by an *adobe*-dwelling friend who claimed facetiously that one of the dirt storms became so violent, when he awoke the following morning he found three extra rooms added to his dwelling. In the North we think of the log cabin as blending with the forest scene, although the situation is reversed. There, the vertical trunks are turned ninety degrees as logs from the vertical to the horizontal to form the log cabin walls.

Just as man has peeled the bark from logs in the construction of his log cabins in order to protect them from insect borers and decay, so has the *adobe* dweller sought to use whatever means at his disposal to protect his materials from erosion. Even today one can on occasion see native women mixing *adobe* and applying it to eroded walls, using their bare hands as trowels. It seems to have been traditionally a woman's work. This comes under the heading of *maintenance*—something we all experience no matter what the dwelling.

To stucco *adobe* walls is to some of the dwellers as abhorrent as the painting of a log cabin would be to that certain cult of deep forest dwellers. But here surely we have diverse opinions. The natural gypsum—a white compound—which can be seen cropping out of the ground in various parts of the Southwest, has traditionally been utilized by the early native to whiten interior walls and in some instances the exteriors as well.

I suppose that one can impose his individuality and fly in the face of all adversity wherever, and at whatever, he chooses, but I gained some moral support in the stuccoing of our *adobe* when I learned of this age-old native use of gypsum. The several rooms of our *adobe* were variously tinted when we took possession, largely pink and blue, but after a few center-floor conferences we decided that color might better be achieved by placing colorful pictures and other items against white walls, which in

The whitening of *adobe* walls has been traditional. Note exposed *adobe* at rear.

turn reflect the light so much better in *adobe* houses, especially when, from long practice, windows are small and few.

How do you go about hanging such things as pictures and a heavy bathroom washbowl on *adobe* walls? Hanging pictures I could at first comprehend since nails can be driven into *adobe,* but what about hanging the washbowl? It proved comparatively simple and practical. The plumber bored holes entirely through the thick *adobe* wall, ran iron bolts through the wall from the outside to the sink and the feat was accomplished. But before inserting the bolts, he gouged out a void in the outside wall, laid in a short length of 2 × 4 lumber in which he had made holes, then first inserted the bolts through the 2 × 4 holes and then through the wall. The piece of 2 × 4 was quickly buried in the wall with a glob of *adobe* mud, this *adobe* fill finally lost from view beneath the stucco finish.

The support-principle gave me notions of what I might do in "hanging" various heavy units, or for bonding supporting members when such supports were needed for hung cabinets. I had to cope a kitchen cabinet to fit against an unplumb and curved wall, but once it was painted with that heavy dripless paint so ideal for interiors, you actually couldn't see where the cabinet ended and the wall began.

If Dorothy L. Pillsbury means that all of these structural problems and the elemental nature of *adobe* soil eventually get to be "surface stuff," I can now bend a little her way, because at last all has merged into a composite, objective whole, where "a philosophy and a song" of *adobe* living have hidden the once-irritating structural grain of sand at the invisible center of the pearl.

My wife and I do not leave the North until midwinter because we are fascinated by the winter wilderness—its snow, cold and special charm. One of my recent books, *Paradise Below Zero,* was devoted to this subject. On snowshoes, garbed in fur-ruffed parkas and mukluks, we adjust to the northern winter elements. Yet, we find that the time spent out-of-doors in sub-zero temperatures on ever-deepening late-winter snows is considerably less than that spent indoors. Contrary to that life, at this writing in early afternoon of late February, the outside doors of our *adobe* here on the Pecos stand wide open. We move through them as readily as from one room to another, while the temperature indoors and out is 68. The result is that we live out-of-doors in New Mexico more hours than indoors. When the chill of the evening desert calls for a cedar or piñon pine fire, even then the doors might remain open for awhile, the open fire in the hearth simulating in a sense the campfire.

To describe the virtues of *adobe* living in specific terms has defied most of us, perhaps for the reason that such descriptions can never be tangibly laid down. They are best expressed in vague superlatives and become evanescent the moment one tries to pin them down for categorical examination. Prose doesn't do a fitting descriptive job, and I can understand why so many writers in frustration have had to resort to poetry or so frequently remain silent in the realm of the intangible.

The author and his wife as Greenhorns in the Southwest.

CHAPTER FOUR

"You Are What You Eat"

The caption of this chapter, gleaned from a vitamin chart, presupposes that dietary culture sets the existential pace of mankind. This concept applied to our present theme might more provincially presuppose that on taking up seasonal residence in the Southwest, we will be destined to undergo some physiological, if not psychological, alteration due to the change in our diet. But after the last half-dozen years or more of seasonal living here, I can announce that red-hot Mexican foods are no longer predominantly the traditional diet of the Southwest. The majority of restaurants serve the same roast beef, steak and chicken, free from chili sauce, featured on menus from British Columbia to Florida. The omnipresent common hamburger holds greater sway by far in the Southwest than *tacos* and *enchiladas*. And here, where "ranch" is the name of the game, we found that the hamburger patty itself, as everywhere else, in the sandwich can be lost under the slice of pickle.

One senses in this pervasion of non-Mexican foods over the Southwest the rather rapid dilution of the Hispanic and Mexican influence, just as we find the dilution of the Dutch influence in Pennsylvania, the Swedish influence in Minnesota, the French in Louisiana, and so on through the whole gamut of ethnic and language provincialism. Mexican restaurants there are, of course, but these will be specialized and primarily in the large centers, as there are universally distributed specialized Italian pizza parlors, Swedish smorgasbords, and the highly lauded specialized French fare, in which without the addition of wine, French cooking would lose its ethnic identity.

The inspiring fragrance of piñon pine.

Some food items, especially chili con carne, the hamburger and the hot dog, have gained such universal favor they are certain to remain as much a staple over the entire continent as apple pie.

In Old Albuquerque, we found La Placita, a restaurant with the highly cosmopolitan food choice to which I have referred. Caught amicably in the folds of the Hispanic-Mexican culture, my wife and I planned to have a La Placita, Mexican dinner. In fact, as we entered, we were of the opinion that our dinner would have to be Mexican cooking or none at all, if we were to judge by the Spanish-Mexican facade. This proved to be illusory. We perused the Mexican regimen of the menu, which offered a generous choice, but we wound up choosing what one might order in Minneapolis, Tulsa, or New York—a medium-rare steak from choice beef raised on grama grass of the Southwestern desert.

The atmosphere of La Placita was, nevertheless, as Mexican as *frijoles*. Its appointments and cultural adornments were impressive. Paintings by Southwestern artists adorned the walls, and these could be bought at a princely sum. If nothing else had identified La Placita with the Southwest, then its geographical location would have become apparent by the gentle, inspiring fragrance of piñon pine burning in open fireplaces.

If the caption of this chapter, *you are what you eat,* is to be taken seriously, then the old adage that when you are in Rome you do what the Romans do, has long lost its original decorum, for one eats in the Southwest pretty much what one eats anywhere. And more—Spanish-speaking Mexican-Americans are as likely in their province to be doing what other Americans do, whether this is culturally or alimentally good or bad.

Some hint of the universality of things expressed in food occurred to me last fall when a guest literally "dropped" in by pontoon plane for a visit at our cabin camp deep in the wilds of northern Canada. As a part of the provision list he had included the luxury of two magnificent wild-blueberry pies, still cold from a freezer. "The only place in the world where you could get a blueberry pie like this is here in a blueberry country," we agreed. (The area is a prolific wild-blueberry region.) My guest explained that the pies had been bought in the supermarket at Sioux Lookout, Ontario. From the wastebasket I dug out the wrapping to nail down for future reference the maker of these excellent pies. There, ironically on the label was the source, "Los Angeles, California."

Despite the cosmopolitan dietary trend, in the Southwest there are Mexican foods, and in great abundance and variety. Perhaps our long-developed palates strange to these foods need just as long cultivation for adjustment. We were already having reservations about the liberal use of chili and a few other condiments that seemed to dominate so much of the Mexican-style food. After some red-hot dishes served to us, we began to look rather askance at the huge red piles of cellophane-packaged chili pepper in the supermarkets. Yet, we toyed with the idea that we might come to like it.

It seemed to us that anything so potent as chili pepper must be imperishable. What bacteria, we thought, good or bad, could possibly live as a culture on dry, powdered chili pepper? This proved wrong. The bag we bought in our brave endeavor to assimilate in our fare a share of this gastronomic TNT after some time began to develop mold. We reconsidered that if chili powder could be affected by mold, it might even break down in the human stomach and digest.

Mrs. Favado, our neighbor down on the Pecos, after hearing our apprehensions regarding Mexican food, convinced us that restaurant Mexican food was not always an epicurean delight. She would prepare a meal of Mexican food, she said, that we would like. My wife offered to resign her kitchen to Mrs. Favado. But gas stoves with temperature-control dials, electric mixers, and other doodads, she pointed out, would only spoil good food. One must have a wood-burning stove, copper or iron pots, a metate and mono (millstones for handgrinding corn) and the *horno* (outdoor, caliche oven). She would start the meal in the morning, we were told, and allow it to cook all day. I was eager to watch every step of so elemental an approach to satisfying the inner man, but she shunted me off by the simple invitation: "You come when the sun goes down."

Not four or five o'clock Mountain Standard Time, but "when the sun goes down"; not stoves with automatic controls, but a wood stove with several square feet of hot cast iron surface where one can make beautiful *tortillas;* not a self-cleaning oven in a gas or electric streamlined range, but the *horno,* the *adobe* oven that bakes bread brown-crusted all around with perfectly uniform heat; not a thin saucepan suspended over a gas flame or an electric element that scorches so easily, but a heavy cast iron pot that simmers evenly, undisturbed on the back of the wood stove; not flour or corn meal which has lost its valuable nutriment by commercial processing, but whole grain, hand-ground in the metate.

I listened to Mrs. Favado, not with compassion for her "primitive" versus modern equipment, but with a shuffling of human values in my mind that left me reflecting throughout the day on the insignificance of what Mrs. Favado had actually lost and what she had gained by not being caught up in the mechanization of today.

That you are not necessarily what you eat is fairly obvious, but that what you eat holds a highly significant place in man's culture and attitude toward life goes, of course, without saying. Mrs. Favado was from the "old school" but, nevertheless, she knew the intricacies of the supermarket, and boasted that she had not fallen under its spell. What her husband brought home in the pickup truck was a far cry from the packaged, processed, monosodium-glutamated, cyclamated, sodium-phosphated items that were carried out of markets by most modern-oriented housewives in a paper bag.

The *cocido* which she cooked and served I would translate into what we would term in the North, a highly sublimated stew. Since it had both fruit and vegetables, both pork and beef, chick peas, seasoned with onion, *orégano,* celery, *comino,* and whatever infusions of flavor that combine, the delicacy she set before us was no doubt a far more sophisticated culinary venture than the stew which in the North has "made me what I am."

If I remember correctly, there were close to twenty ingredients in the *cocido.* Mrs. Favado said that it was the chief dish of Spanish-Mexicans. Though she had prepared it the day we dined with her, I cannot imagine *cocido* as being a staple menu for everyday consumption, unless basically it was limited to the simple stew or mulligan ingredient of the North. Stew-accumulatus cannot be reduced to a formula, for stew is never the same from one cycle of accumulation to another. I, therefore, must believe that elemental life in old New Mexico might center around the stew pot, but only as the accumulating leftovers multiplied to family appetite capacity.

Cocido? On the festive occasion, of course.

Anyone who serves stew the first day that it is prepared has inadvertently left out the most important ingredient—blending. There must be a true relationship between every item in the pot. Only time will do this. Mrs. Favado displayed a sympathetic rationalization here. She agreed with me that while her *cocido* was as good as we told her it was, tomorrow it would be much better, and she put all of it that we didn't eat in a screw-top jar for us to reheat after it had the mellowing benefit of time.

I asked Mrs. Favado and her husband what they would buy as provisions from the supermarket, if they were to start from scratch. The answer came readily from Mr. Favado, "You start by buying a hundred pounds of flour, a hundred pounds of potatoes, fifty pounds of onions, and twenty-five pounds of sugar. From now on you can pick and choose according to your pocketbook."

Can it be that in austerity there is the seed of great wisdom? We asked Mrs. Favado how she cooked *frijoles* (pinto beans). *Frijoles* by now had inescapably captured and held us as a recurrent staple fare. Mrs. Favado went through the various steps, from selecting fresh beans raised at proper mountain elevation to picking them over, washing and simmering them in (and this was important) rainwater for hours, adding the salt only after considerable cooking, and then adding some *lard*. The addition of lard disturbed us. "Wouldn't it be better, Mrs. Favado," we asked, "to add bacon or ham instead of lard?"

"Sometimes you have bacon," she said, "and sometimes you don't."

Austerity? It can be grim, but perhaps a necessary, profound experience.

We later cooked some pintos as Mrs. Favado had recommended, but left out the lard or bacon. Without doubt, if you don't have bacon, we learned, pintos do need lard. Whenever we cooked pinto beans thereafter, adding not lard, not bacon, but the luxury of ham or smoked pork chops, we had the guilt of extravagance and thought of Mrs. Favado and Mexican austerity.

The true value of lard, however, was brought home to me in my earlier travels through the Canadian wilderness. I had accompanied a Royal Canadian Mounted Policeman on a regional patrol to supply a lard complement both to Indians and non-Indians who had suffered malnutrition as a result of the caribou herd having failed in its migration to show up in a particular forested region. The Indians had been reduced to a diet of snowshoe hares. The hare is good sustaining food, but deficient in fat. A complement of lard is needed and the Mountie and I had two dogsled loads of packaged lard to distribute.

One of our stops was at a white trapper's cabin. Though a man of less than fifty years, he was known as "Old Doughnuts." He had always stored up a vast number of doughnuts as soon as cold enough weather had set in to freeze them. When the caribou herd failed to come through, he lived on snowshoe hares and doughnuts. The fat complement here had made his snowshoe hares highly sustaining, and he laughed at our concern for his welfare, serving us coffee and doughnuts.

The pinto bean. Has it been properly exalted? What is so extraordinary about it? Proof that the pinto is not just an ordinary bean—try placing a pot of navy beans and water on the stove to simmer for several hours. What do you come up with? An insipid mess. They must have the complement of onion, mustard, molasses, tomato sauce, pork and what not, then baked in order to bridge over this insipidity. The navy bean then becomes the *Boston baked bean* and is, I grant, delectable. But what is so delectable about it—the mustard, onion, molasses, tomato flavoring? Mostly, but, of course, in complement with the beans.

Now, simmer some pintos in water for several hours; better, simmer them all day on the back of Mrs. Favado's wood stove. Not much happens the first hour. Gradually, the water begins to turn a rich brown. As cooking proceeds, a delectable sauce is exuded from the pintos which in time thickens into a creamy brown-gravy consistency. One needs the lard, the bacon or the smoked pork chops, of course, to top off the end result, but the bean even without the meat has supplied its own rich flavoring, garnishing itself, so to speak.

The government in its anxiety over the Southwestern Indian baby being nurtured beyond the mother's milk without ample cow's milk, sought to look into the matter of malnutrition. Well, there wasn't much to fret about. The rich sauce from the pinto bean had most of what a baby needs. The early Southwest Indian raised squash and pinto beans and these took care of a large share of his nutritional needs. The wild land afforded numerous food complements, but when it did not, the pinto bean with its high protein and other food values bridged the dietary gap.

The greenhorn on first entering the Southwest sees Spanish-Mexican cookery fundamentally as a kind of exotic epicurism, a food culture, confusing to his hunger after a few thousand miles of aiming his late-model car down the regimented highway. Back in North Dakota, Pennsylvania or Maine, he has listened with apprehension to talk about the chili-hot foods on which he must fare when he reaches the Southwest. *Tortillas, enchiladas* or *tacos* seem to be his first experience. He sticks the point of his fork in the hot sauce and, with a highly communicable smile across the table, says, "WOW!"

In that "Wow," we have the basis of most Mexican cooking. There are the other spices—*chimajá* (wild cherry), *yerba buena* (wild mint), *culantro* (coriander), *orégano* (wild marjoram) found and used pretty much anywhere on the continent (or over the world), but underlying the Mexican-Spanish cooking is *chili.* If you begin with *caldo colado* (clear soup), move on to pea, bean or tomato soup, ride hungrily into entrees of oysters, pot roast, a chicken stewed in sherry, or a boiled dinner, there is the ever-dominant chili powder or pulp.

It has generally been the theory of great cooks that seasoning should never impose. It must be so delicately balanced in a recipe that only the highly-trained chef could discover that it was used at all. It should be like appropriate background music in a theatre—of high complement but not conspicuously in evidence or obtrusive on the drama itself.

Chili?

In the Spanish-Mexican foods it dominates, it overwhelms, it rides rampant over the palate and obscures the taste of whatever variety of ingredients form the vehicle on which it rides, like a wild horse with the reins thrown to abandon over its head. Some foods, I admit, are so free from condiments it is like riding a dead horse with the reins held firmly in one's grip, but one might ask that the horse be under control, where gastronomy sits comfortably in the saddle.

Leave out chili powder or chili pulp from Spanish-Mexican recipes and you couldn't tie down its geographical identity on land or sea. But, now and then, as some like a sharp whiskey burn, I prefer to sweat my forehead with chili, and what basic food it dominates doesn't make a hell of a lot of difference. With the fire of this spice I use the word *hell* advisedly.

CHAPTER FIVE

A Day at Home in the Southwest

Anthropology has thrown some interesting light on early man's distribution over the earth and how he has been affected by differences in environment. But not much thought has been given by science toward the effect on modern man's environmental change through the medium of modern rapid transportation. Sporadic visits far and wide will, of course, have little significant effect. But the environmental effect on the seasonal migrant could prove to be a highly revealing physiological and psychological study. We have gained some data on the effect which temperature and humidity have upon man. A neighbor in the North who has built a home in Florida, for example, speaks highly of the Florida climate and scene except for one deleterious aspect. The humid warmth, he says, is dulling to the physical spirit, and he thinks, incidentally to mental vigor. A retired Columbia University professor made a study of intellectual enterprise as influenced by temperature. He found a difference of about 60 percent in the intellectual achievement factor of cold over hot climates, and noted that while heat is conducive to growth, it does not as readily incubate ideas. In the moderate New Mexico desert winter we have found a temperature-influence compromise.

Different from tourist travel, the seasonal resident picks up his whole domestic process about every three to six months and sets it down in a completely different environment. This length of time in a changed environment could have a noteworthy effect.

There was a time when we regarded our principal home as being Marine on St. Croix, Minnesota, a tiny village considered outer-suburbia to Minneapolis and St. Paul. For a time we departed from there seasonally for a cabin in the north woods. Canadians refer to such places as "camps." And that, essentially, is what it was, merely a diversion from a more or less conventional button-pushing life. Zoning ordinances for tax advantages to the state and several other factors have altered the cabin concept until we can no longer regard one particular place as our main home. Our dwelling in the Southwest where we spend about three months at the "tail end" of the winter, our dwelling on the shore of Lake Superior where we escape the top heat of summer, now unavoidably have become fully appointed, modern domestic "spreads." The only exception is a remote cabin we have in the northern Ontario, Canada, wilderness, but even here we are restricted to a more pretentious structure than we needed or wanted in order to "prove up" on a provincial cabin site.

About three months in each of the places mentioned cannot, of course, lay down a basis, I realize, for studying the effect of environment upon our physiological and intellectual processes. But I am inclined to believe that it does effect an apparent change.

Competition in material goods, food, hardware and dry goods, of all kinds, naturally places just about the same current stock everywhere in the country with but a few variations. One might hope for a less monolithic distribution of all these items for the novelty and cultural change that it would afford. But on the other hand, standard trade names do save one a lot of time in selection. Sara Lee coffee cake, for example, appears in just about every supermarket freezer on the continent, and this is a help, because our experience has been that most bake shops and the current large bread and roll distributors regard the mention of such ingredients as fresh creamery butter, milk and eggs in a roll dough as a form of commercial heresy. That the Sara Lee firm had the integrity and good sense to use these enriching ingredients is commendable. It was bound to become a hundred-million-dollar business. Similarly, one can pick a ham, a can of coffee or other item from a case simply by the long-time stamp of approval one builds up for certain quality-proven trade names.

Outside of the slight variation of foodstuffs mentioned in the chapter "You Are What You Eat," the daily fare thus becomes pretty much the same general variety in the Southwest as anywhere else on the continent.

Beyond this, perhaps, it can be said that the whole pattern of daily life undergoes change.

When we arrive in the Southwest about mid-January, winter, as we know it in the North, with a snow accumulation that remains until the spring breakup, seems strangely left behind. We do get an occasional snowfall on the Southwest desert which usually melts off the following day. A ready heating plant is, therefore, essential, but we give the plant less use, I think, than most. Down sleeping robes, so familiar to us in the North, allow us to keep the doors open at night, merely screened from insects and rodents. When the morning sun rolls up over the mesa across the Pecos and sends its warming rays through the two front doors, we become alive to the day, close the doors, and touch a match to the piñon pine kindling made ready in the Franklin fireplace stove the night before. This is the moment when my wife turns over, peers sleepily into the flames and remarks, "My, what a nice fire."

What this actually means to her, translated, is, "Now I had better get up and put on the coffee pot." There is something imminent about this. It stemmed from the time that, by example, I made coffee late at night to be stored in a vacuum bottle for immediate consumption in the morning, so as not having to wait until after a shower, grooming and other cosmetic preliminaries so time-consuming by the fair sex, before a cup of coffee would be available. She now performs with incredible wifely expedience. The Pyrex percolator with its complex "innards," even with a cellulose filter, poses conveniently on a shelf ready for action. My own "gunsmoke" coffee (a handful of coffee tossed into a pot of boiling water) might do for the trail, but not by her standards where any semblance of a conventional roof overhead is available. We have the Pyrex combinations at all four places in four cup and larger capacities, and I learned early that extra glass "innards," replacing those that get broken in the dishwashing, are highly conducive to domestic bliss.

Thus the day starts with the amalgamated fragrance of burning piñon pine, clear desert air, and percolating coffee. Our schedule for the day, if there is a schedule at all, is not *mañana** exactly, but we do have our

---

*Tomorrow. Humorously interpreted as meaning, "Don't do today what you can put off until tomorrow," and suggests things never getting done.

While the coffee perks, I make the run to the post office.

breakfast in leisure before the open fire. While the coffee perks, I make the mile and a quarter run with the "Carry-All" to the post office for the mail. Consuming the last cup of coffee becomes a protracted affair while we open, read and comment on the mail. Mail quite often determines what the day will bring.

From my readers I get a strange variety of requests. Oddly, a great deal of the mail does not apply at all to information contained in my publications. Some readers want to know how they might make a living in the wilderness, others ask for escape formulas to "the best of two worlds." There is a considerable amount of this escape mail. Writers, for some strange reason, are believed to have an advantageous insight on life. I wish that I had. It might solve a few of my own perplexities.

One does, however, get from this mail an opportunity to learn where one's books go, who reads them, and what the reader reaction is. One of the financial statements from my publisher, for instance, showed that a quantity of my books on the wilderness had gone to Yugoslavia. Obviously, Tito, I concluded, had taken to the woods. Perhaps, the most important mail that I get is from young people, some so young their letters appear to have been written by bearing down hard on stubby pencils. I treat their requests with special regard, for here surely lie most potentials in possibly rehabilitating a ravaged world.

Northerners visiting the Southwest are impressed by the rapid rise in temperature from early morning toward noon. A morning temperature of 40 in the North can, of course, on occasion rise appreciably by noon, but generally substantial rises do not obtain. On the Southwest desert a slow rise would be the exception. I have no scientific explanation for the rapid rise, and can only presume that since the New Mexican atmosphere is extremely clear—haze being at a minimum—the sun's power to warm the air and earth is considerably greater than in areas of higher humidity.

An hour after the sun rises, the temperature from a night desert reading of 40 reaches well into the 50s, and by noon rises enough to impart a feeling of summer warmth. The typewriter gets moved out on the patio, which I think is a mistake because the early morning light playing fantastic shadow-shapes on the distant mesas, the Pecos flowing gently below, a mule deer perhaps grazing on the alfalfa, cañon towhees and piñon jays feeding in the yard—these are all too delightfully distracting to allow one to get lost in writing which may not pertain to the immediate scene.

As I remember, George Jean Nathan, the theatrical critic, famous as the partner with H. L. Mencken in publication of the controversial American Mercury, used to do his writing by first sharpening a fistful of lead pencils and then turning his desk toward a blank wall while he wrote. Even looking out over a busy city through a New York apartment or office window, it seemed, diverted his thoughts too much to other subjects, away from the theme of immediate need. This seems plausible because my most conscientious work is done when I retreat to our combination guest and studio cabin, while a sandstorm blackens the air outside to the exclusion of all but my inner thoughts.

No responsible duty to the "establishment" induces us to give up the hours from after lunch to sundown away from recreation in the Pecos Valley, off in some other canyon, or atop a distant mesa. Through February as the sun's declination climbs, we keep telling each other that the near summer warmth of sunshine that floods the scene before us is taking place while the North is caught in the throes of accumulated snow and increasing sub-zero temperatures.

What we seek and what we find in these afternoon sallies is principally the New Mexican wilderness. Yet, it can be said that we never get to know the full meaning of wilderness. It is too inscrutable, too mystifying, too caught up with millions of years and the effects of the millennial time processes. In hiking over the untrammeled areas of New Mexico, there is more a feeling of treading on a dry ocean floor. Wilderness? The very essence of the word mystifies thought. The profound aspects of the wilderness can reach only those who have not yet been numbed by the ossifying urban effect in the scramble for material gain. Perhaps we need to redefine from time to time the terms *wilderness* and *civilization* to fit the rapid mutations of both.

There is, I feel, a nostalgia in our present-day outlook on the wilderness—a strong desire to repossess that which seems tragically on the wane. Unfortunately, there are no accessible planets possessing the natural phenomena of the earth offering an alternative escape, otherwise we might seek to keep such a planet inviolate from man's industrial depredations, and allow the best of his faculties and optimum physical welfare to flourish there. Nevertheless, we are grateful for the alternative we have gained from the urban sprawl—an opportunity to lose ourselves in the remaining micro-wilderness areas, at least those having retained, as in the New Mexican wilds, some semblance of the natural, uncontaminated, original earth.

Fortunately, the Pecos Canyon for about twenty-five miles below our dwelling is almost devoid of land suitable for irrigation. This is environmentally good fortune. Cattle, of course, range freely over the rough terrain, but with an average of 40 acres allocated to the mother cow, one sees the herd only at rare intervals. If, during those intervals, we do not

At such times we sit on the rim of the canyon and allow the wilderness intimately to absorb us.

hear a plane passing overhead, there can be a silent majesty in the valley that is little different from what the environment might have been a thousand years ago. At such times, we are apt to sit on the rim of a canyon and simply allow the wilderness intimately to absorb us.

There is, most of the time, an all-pervading solitude which might imply that no natural mutations are taking place. But this we know is not so. We know that if we could compress a million years into one, the change would be so phenomenal before our eyes, it would be a thundering, frightful mutation. What a refreshing spectacle if we could sit atop a mountain and watch a reverse compression of time correcting the past and present depredations and defilements of man, see Eden, as it were, springing up where the ravage of nature has been the order of "progress."

Sitting on the edge of some canyon, we frequently find great pleasure in idle conjecture—sometimes wild conjecture but perhaps fairly within the compass of reasonable rational soundness. One phase of this is the basic concept that complete environmental destruction per se might be a misnomer. We have considered, for example, that the forces, processes and elements of the earth, the ecosystems, are actually never destroyed. No matter how we pollute and charge fresh water with foreign substances, crystal clear water can again be taken from it by evaporation and other processing. We may ravage at will, but should it so happen that man by some holocaust, nuclear or otherwise, eliminated himself as a species entirely from the earth, the natural forces would go to work, reestablish the ecocycles, and rehabilitate the earth to what it was with no great variation before man managed his depredations. This would take time, but irrespective of man's brief life span, what is a million years in the earth's mutations?

When we realize that various governments have been so constituted that a single individual could set off a nuclear war and reduce the world population to a fragmentary minimum or to complete extinction, the hypothesis is not too farfetched. In fact, if I may be allowed another extravagant conjecture, I am quite certain that one or the other—complete extinction or near extinction of humanity—will someday occur. The potential of a nuclear force is too choice a weapon to escape the opportunism of some ideological maniac. Or, pollution in itself may as likely work such havoc.

The millions of years that would necessarily have to follow such a catastrophe before the earth could again be set back in order through its natural rehabilitation processes, seems incomprehensible. As we observe the phenomena around us from our seat on the rim of the canyon, we are looking at one phase of a geological process that has already taken millions of years. It is only man's ephemeral existence on earth which makes a few million years seem chronologically incredible.

One might presume that such sojourns into these wilderness areas of New Mexico and their resultant conjectures might tend to make us intemperate, and that we should rather be getting the nerve therapy that inviolate nature provides. This might be a fair conclusion except that in our conjectures we are merely playing the devil's advocate and doing it with tongue in cheek and much amusement, despite the potential possible seriousness of such conjectures actually someday becoming reality. Much of the time we lie in the sun, soaking it up, while a gentle muse occupies our thoughts; or we snoop and prod into the mysteries and miracles of the local natural phenomena. One thing is quite certain: it is nigh impossible to become too apprehensive over the frets of man while in a wilderness environment. At least we don't fret the small stuff of conventional blunders. Somehow the perspective one gains in a remote wilderness region allows very little significance to be attached to the problems of the urban establishment. Importance of the grand industrial plan diminishes in proportion to one's appreciation and focus upon nature.

The return to our *adobe* dwelling from these jaunts might be described as a *saunter*. Supper, a few hours with a good book before a piñon pine fire, possibly an hour or two lying blanketed on the patio cots watching the incredibly beautiful desert sky, or an evening with friends, round out the day. It is on the desert alone where the concept of light-year distances do not apply. Stars come down in a vast scintillating mantle, seeming barely out of reach. As a long-time student of celestial navigation in my wilderness travels, about fifty of the stars have become intimate "guideposts." We are far enough south to note that some of them which seem well above the horizon in the North, here in the Southwest ride just above the river mesas.

Tomorrow, we may be in Santa Fe, Taos or Albuquerque, at the Grand Canyon, perhaps riding a quarter horse most anywhere, or ferreting out some interesting individual whom we are told, we "ought to meet." Exploring unusual minds, as biographers have shown, can be as fascinating as a trek into some unexamined, untrammeled area. But exploring other minds often boomerangs—a case of getting explored ourselves. Still, if one has anything at all to offer, what can be more noble than intellectual reciprocity?

CHAPTER SIX

On Poking Around

February and March of each year can scarcely be regarded as time or season enough to gain an indigenous foothold in New Mexico, or anywhere for that matter. For three years we were content to leave for the North to see the winter breakup in Minnesota. But last year we decided to remain in New Mexico long enough to observe the Pecos Valley burst into its full vernal splendor.

Warm New Mexican days with temperatures sometimes as high as the 70s during January and February would seem mild enough for vegetation to sprout, but the nights at 40° or colder and little precipitation hold most growth seasonally dormant. The leafless gray drabness of vegetation that early May suggests in the North, prevails through February and March in New Mexico—an April first impression we carried off on our annual north-bound departure for three successive years.

In March, though temperatures rise substantially in New Mexico, the earth gives little promise of fertility. George Gissing in his book, *The Private Papers of Henry Ryecroft,* exclaimed, "Oh, for only one more spring!" We had hoped to see three springs in a single year: New Mexico's, Minnesota's, and Canada's burst into bloom at different times, succeeding one another in the order given, but our latitudinal calculations were not to be borne out. Spring rains come late in the Southwest. We discovered that a Minnesota spring breaks out about as soon as New Mexico's. Could one not, with Ryecroft's yearnings live with perpetual spring by moving along the sun's vernal course? Apparently not. Nevertheless, we stayed in New Mexico long enough to return to Minnesota with an impression of the Southwest that was more like a sun-splashed, lush oasis.

While emphasis throughout this book is on wilderness, the reader will obviously be aware that residence largely has been chosen where one hand reaches out to a natural, more or less inviolate region, while the other hand is extended to the warmth of humanity. The *adobe* on the Pecos lies eleven miles from Santa Rosa; the cabin on Lake Superior thirty-one miles from Thunder Bay, Ontario, Canada; our principal home on the St. Croix River less than an hour's drive from the twin metropolis of Minneapolis and St. Paul. The fourth place, a cabin twenty-five miles from a road on Canada's Precambrian shield, might seem to alter the wilderness and humanity aspect, but air transportation here by bush pilots using pontoon landing on water and ski landing in winter, has changed earlier concepts of remoteness. Nevertheless, withal, when night falls, a serenity prevails at each place that is manifestly nonurban. Perhaps the quietness that comes over the desert emphasizes this fact the most.

Wherever one establishes a living place, it is obviously not only the immediate confines of the purchased property that one considers. In a broad possessive sense, one acquires virtually the entire radial environment. In New Mexico we reason that along with the land and cabin, we bought such attributes as the Pecos River and a wilderness canyon with their various natural assets; the Sangre de Cristo Mountain Range rising over 13,000 feet; a sun that shines 85 percent of the time, and not only provides physical benefits but also gives fantastic morning and evening lightings to mesa and canyon walls; uncontaminated air; a good road to market and library, winding for ten miles through a picturesque canyon that never fails to inspire; and no less the alluring desert. No deed in fee simple to these acquired values, of course, though when we received the title to our property, we liked to think that all of the named attributes were sort of generously thrown in for good measure.

At times we have reflected on the possibility that our seasonal change in environment may be too often. Indigenous tap roots that long living in an environment send down into the ground, make it impossible for some people ever to move away from their native homes. And we become more and more aware that the small rootlets which we as seasonal residents send into the shallower ground create some despair as well in the frequent transplant. The abrupt seasonal cutoff has its increasing nostalgia.

GREENHORNS IN THE SOUTHWEST

Then, there are the quail in the yard.

One season we are looking across the scattered chaparral of the desert range.

The next, we find ourselves retraining our eyes across Northern wilderness water.

From season to season we build up a warm attachment to the people around us in whatever seasonal place we happen to occupy. Life becomes interlaced and increasingly complex. In time, as familiarity and mutual advantages grow, one sees moist eyes on the departure, and the best histrionic front one can assume on such occasions is but a poor piece of emotional concealment. Every year the embrace and the parting remarks, "We will see you next year," and "Be sure to write often," get to be more difficult.

Then, there are the quail in the yard that we have been feeding, the cañon towhees, white crowned sparrows, the roadrunner, and the rest. The last day in seasonal residence, the remaining stock of ground feed and maize gets dumped out on the ground and into feeding hoppers. It is a mere remorseful gesture because we know it won't last too many days. These guests who so delighted us, will keep coming and find that hospitality has ceased.

Thus, one season we are looking across the scattered chaparral of the desert range; the next, we find ourselves in an environment where we have to retrain our eyes across Northern wilderness water to high-rising forests, and follow woodland portage trails around roaring caldrons of thundering rivers. It takes time to make the many adjustments, but despite the various reactions, we convince ourselves that environmental and social change is desirable.

New Mexico is a place where we have come to enjoy life in the present and hope to project it as far into the future as life's time allotment will provide. But New Mexico is also a place where one's interest must be projected into the past. The frontier epochs in which New Mexico is so rich are unavoidable chapters. The reminders are at every turn of the back-country roads, in every canyon. Ghost towns stand grim and haunting, dozing in their twilight sleep on the old dusty roads. They silently suggest, "Once upon a time . . ." No great play of the imagination is necessary to restore them to where they live again with their frontier populations, eager for the life that came and is now gone, each having played out its hour of glory. The ghost town hitching rail in front of the saloon is still intact but without its horses patiently dozing. An air of utter abandonment is felt, especially when a windblown tumbleweed rolls down the

Ghost towns stand grim and haunting.

street. The bar, covered with dust from sandstorms blown through sagging doors, serves no beer or whiskey, features no saloon girls. Those who lived there seem like phantoms. Yet, the least regeneration of image by the play of imagination allows all of the earlier human contact, gaiety, sensualism, rowdyism, and serious living to return before one's conjured-up gaze, and suddenly the feeling of mystery no longer lingers within the ghostly structural remnants.

Upon entering a bedroom of a very old *adobe* house, the wind blowing through it attracted our attention to the flapping pages of a coverless copy of Dostoevski's *Crime and Punishment*—a Spanish translation published in Barcelona, Spain, in 1903.

In the streets of ghost towns, old wagon tongues and wheels lie bleaching in the desert sun. Some have divested themselves of nearly all of their wood, the iron rims and hub parts hanging more durably onto tradition by their greater material resistance to the elements, lying half-buried in the dry wind-shifting soil. Weary porch posts, leaning, seem ready to topple. Doors stand open, banging against their walls, buffeted by the wind.

The history of these ghost towns is not projected so far in the past but what we can extract from actual records in most instances when and why the early settlers first established and finally abandoned them. One can usually estimate from the condition of the roofs approximately how long ago the towns were abandoned. The roof is the most vulnerable part in the decay process. Just a small leak of rain allows enough moisture to enter a structure and be contained within to expedite this roof-wrecking decay, though outside the environment may be dry as talcum powder. Rafters in time rot and break from the trapped moisture, the roof finally collapsing within the structure, and the struggle to remain goes into its last throes.

"Now," says nature, "the walls." If the walls are *adobe,* they dissolve from rains and wind erosion, growing gradually thinner and lower until they are returned to the desert soil from whence they came. If of stone and *adobe* mortar, gravity and wind topple the highest stones, then the next highest, and so on until only rectangular stone piles remain to delineate the approximate position of the original walls. Given time, these will be eroded out of existence, until only the most trained archaeologist will be able to trace and identify the wall positions of a once human habitation. I often wonder what New York or London would look like after a million years, were it, along with its people, destroyed by a nuclear holocaust and not restored.

It is the stone structures, the rubble remains with about half of the walls still standing or others with scarcely a trace of the original structure, that tend to arouse one's speculation about the life that went on here in the desert centuries ago. All trace of the wooden *vigas* that supported a dirt roof have disappeared. The lower portion of the door openings in many of these ruins can still be identified. The origin of the older ruins greatly transcends the more recent ghost towns in age. Earlier ruins did not, of course, set in towns. Older ruins usually are located along rivers, near a spring, or at a large, water-trapping pool below the drop of some rock-bound arroyo. Invariably the ruins command a good view of a valley or other approach. The view, judging from its location, was not chosen wholly for aesthetic reasons, though beauty and the cooling effect of breezes were, I am sure, as important to these early people as they are to us today. What seems most evident is that the camps needed to command a view where an enemy could not easily come upon its occupants from ambush, and this seems to be invariably the situation. Where there is no evidence of old shelters, but where the elevation suggests a strategic camp area, we usually find artifacts.

To some extent, of course, we can equate the lives lived in the desert ghost towns with our own. One tries to conjure up the naturalistic life lived in the small stone structures, which are now little more than rubble. I have often sat nearby in quiet contemplation of this early life, trying to conjecture from the general nature of the environment, the ruins and the artifacts, what the aspirations, the joys and sorrows, births and deaths might have been here, for we, after all, are their prototypes.

A kind of mathematics is needed, I think. One starts subtracting: No industrial wheels turned in naturalistic man's life, though a kind of naturalistic industry or culture obviously was carried on. There was the fletching of arrows, the grinding of beans and other seeds for flour in a metate, the smoking of meat, the making of baskets and pottery, and the tanning of hides for fashioning clothes. If one regards these various activities as crude, one needs to reconsider. Indian tanned skins can be as soft as velvet. Artifacts show exceptional skill and much decorative art. That much of the craft was a labor of love is obvious. I never cease to be inspired when in a ruin or cave I find a piece of ancient pottery that has been artistically decorated, for I know that life then was not so grim but what an effort was made toward embellishment—toward ennoblement of the spirit.

While there was then no medical profession to reduce a patient to poverty in time, there was a kind of therapeutics, and if not nearly as comprehensive as in modern-day treatment, then at least there was a compensatory healthful life and activity in the open that reduced clinical needs to a minimum. There was no thousand-dollar surgery, but there were people in the tribe who could set a broken limb and suture a severed tendon. (In my earlier travels in the Far North, I found where an Eskimo's broken kneecap had been repaired, the surgery done by the women.) The naturalistic man, no doubt, would have welcomed the benefits of modern surgery when he needed them, but he lived without them—in some cases less advantageously, in others probably more.

To continue the subtraction: Naturalistic man had no lifetime home mortgage to pay off, no industrial servitude, no income taxes, no pollution of air and water, no continual economic or conventional sword of Damocles hanging daily over his head. True, there must have been periods of famine, but the desert then still inviolate generally provided, and starvation, we can conclude from the desert supply, was no more common than it is today in many parts of our industrial and agricultural world.

New Mexico boasts a much older human habitation by far than that suggested by the rubble of small stone shelters, scientific dating methods having now projected this habitation back beyond any heretofore concepts of man's origin.

When we established our fourth residence in the New Mexican desert, a strange awareness crept over us that we were to settle in the very region where the San Jon (pronounced Hone) Man, the Sandia Man, and the Folsom Man likely had trodden.

In 1917, the Smithsonian Institution examined the San Jon region and found an arrow point different from any other, naming it the San Jon point. They also found the skull of a Phytosaur, prepared it for shipment, and discovered that the crated skull alone weighed nearly a thousand pounds. The San Jon area takes on a special significance therefore when it is realized that this plant-eating lizard lived in a period about two hundred million years ago.

These are some of the fibers out of which the Southwest historical and prehistorical pattern is woven. New Mexico has not been lax in the consolidation of its historical and scientific material. As greenhorns, we, of course, have available the same academic sources for learning about the Southwest that any area provides for its region: books, people, museums, and, firsthand, the land itself and the actual finding of artifacts which the soil exposes by erosion. We have seen that the Southwest has become not only the focus and interest of its own people, but the focus and interest of the whole scientific world. San Jon, Sandia, and Folsom Man findings have aroused the scientific world in fixing the evolution of man beyond preconceived beliefs, complementing other proof round the world in the archaeological search for man's true origin.

Our cabin on the Pecos has, perhaps, demanded less provinciality than any other of the four places we occupy seasonally. We find a rich local, natural and cultural interest here as indicated, but places beyond the immediate area become more and more alluring each year. Taos and Santa Fe, with their community of artists and writers, hold a highly sustaining cultural attraction. The mountains being so varied in general nature from the desert—and because of the change in vegetation and wildlife that altitude alone provides—we cannot resist botanizing and mammalizing a bit over the entire Southwest on every altitude level, reaching some remote areas only by foot, saddle and pack horse. Archaeological search is, of course, ever dominant in our minds and for a large share of the population here. The Southwest by its archaeological nature offers the most productive study of man's origin on the continent. Museums and art galleries lure us off over highways we might ordinarily not travel.

Though a tendency to roam wider with each season increases, our immediate backyard interests are not neglected. As greenhorns in the Southwest who boast an avid interest in the outdoors by long association and having acquired a smattering of Northern Wilderness knowledge, we might in time be held responsible to some degree by associates for acquired naturalistic knowledge here in the Southwest. We, therefore, stay on a sort of crash, bone-up program that never ceases to hold our interest.

The baits and lures that will bring some of the Southwest wild creatures to our back yard have not been wholly successful, though we have not done too badly on a hundred-pound sack of finely ground, mixed feed and another of barley and maize.

Coveys of from thirty to fifty Gambel's and Scaled Quail have apparently found the grain as palatable as desert seeds. Their plumed and tufted crowns give them a most regal appearance. Cañon towhees, scrub and piñon jays, mountain bluebirds, Oregon juncos, white-crowned sparrows, and others are continually feeding on this grain in the yard through the winter months. Mule deer feed on our irrigated alfalfa crop. Now and then, a roadrunner, New Mexico's state bird, shows up to indulge his appetite in a raw chicken egg enticingly set out for him, but he hasn't found domestic food sufficiently attractive to forego entirely his staple diet of snakes, lizards, and the like, to keep him around. Hamburger was suggested as bait. It did not bring in a roadrunner more often, but attracted our erstwhile acquaintance of the North, *mephitis,* the striped skunk. While he appears to have fared quite well on small rodents, bird's eggs, cactus fruits and grubs, he seems to prefer our hamburger and table scraps. He does not fully trust us so far, nor do we exactly trust him. Yet, we have suddenly come upon him on our patio at night within a few feet, with no dire consequences. Perhaps he has already gratefully learned the source of his new diet and prefers to be valorous rather than odorous.

For some time now, table scraps have been placed in a large canned-ham tin, set well out into the yard each night. By morning it is empty. By playing a spotlight on the tin, we have created a center of never-ceasing interest. Three striped skunks and five one-time domestic cats gone wild compete for the table scraps, with confrontations that show a real respect for one another by all opponents. The antics displayed by both the skunks and the cats have become highly amusing. The skunks, apparently, do not consider the cats too contestable, since the skunks have not seen fit so far, at least during our observation, to use their most formidable weapon.

While our four places of residence have great merit from the standpoint of diversion, we have asked ourselves at times, how diversified can one be? At any rate, how encompassing? The world may be getting relatively smaller in size every day, but certainly not in scope. An individual's capacity for gaining knowledge of the world's interminable natural subjects does not expand proportionately. By now, we have come to regard the four living places as a mother would her offspring. Our love for them all is so possessive we cannot conceive of anything so drastic as to give up a single one of them, and this last acquired residence in the Southwest has captured our affections as much as our "first-born" in the North.

CHAPTER SEVEN

"Ranchero"

The inescapable theme in New Mexico's desert is obviously "ranchero." Our ranch cabin is as bound-round literally with barbed wire as the prickly cactus, though we have added wooden planks between the wires on the fence around the cabin to give it less a look of barbed wire severity and more a ranchlike corral effect. It is not unusual for us to awake in the morning and find a virtual sea of beef, the animals pressing curiously against this corral-type fence. An hour later not a single critter of the whole vast herd may be in sight. They will have moved a mile back into the box canyon or dispersed on many distant segments of the far-off, rugged range, not to be seen again perhaps for days or even weeks.

We do not own cattle, but, nevertheless, have developed a range consciousness and possessiveness for those owned by our lessee. A Brahma cow which was about to drop a calf became the focus of our interest for some time. With her high shoulder hump and long, floppy ears, she suggests a water buffalo. Since her sire was a Black Angus, and the Brahma is grayish-white, we were anxious to see what the hybrid result would be. The combination resulted in a species locally dubbed *Brangus*. The calf turned out to be a light-colored gray male with the most extraordinary black streaks across its face. At birth the mother hid it in a remote nook, well up in a rockbound canyon.

One cannot help but wonder at the helplessness of the newborn human as compared to that of the bovine, the deer, and many other animals. Within a few minutes after birth the bovine calf struggles to its feet and begins its first meal. It must have its mother's milk soon after birth or perish, and it gets up on its feet to feed.

The instinct of animal birth and subsequent care always amazes. How the Brahma cow knew that she would be dropping a calf, her first, and what told her to seek some warm, safe, sunlit place out of the wind for the birth, gives one need to wonder about the miracle of informative instinct.

The mother will have an urgent need for a drink of water a day or so after the birth, but she will first nurse her calf and leave it well fed before she herself will go alone to the distant river for a drink. Immediately upon having a drink, she returns dutifully to her offspring. On such departure she may find that coyotes or a mountain lion has, in the short interval, killed the calf and eaten a share. But most often the calf will survive where the mother dropped it and one of these days the calf will also come down the intricate trail from the desert canyon alongside its mother to see the river world.

Tragedy can strike in various ways at time of birth. A neighboring rancher found that vultures had picked out the eyes of a mother cow while she was helplessly giving birth to her calf. Such advantage taken of a mother at this time seems cruel in nature beyond belief. By resection in the above incident the calf, however, was removed and it lived, though the mother had to perish in the process.

Despite man's place in the animal kingdom, he cannot fully grasp what underlies the behavior pattern of what he likes to call the lower animals. Man attaches a reasoning capability to himself but insists that some unreasoning routine regulates the behavior of all other animal life, and conveniently places it in the neat category of *instinct.* This instinct concept he applies to animals below and above his own natural capabilities, which, if they were possessed by man, he would regard as reasoning powers, or superior human perceptions. If we could truly define the terms *reason* and *instinct* for differentiation, we might find so much overlap, the broad distinction now held between the two terms might well begin to narrow, or vanish as a scientific concept.

I prefer to think of animal behaviorism as quite superior to what we derogatively refer to in common as "only instinct." Yesterday, for

These newly born calves, unfamiliar with water, waded across the river as though having done it through long practice.

example, we saw the birth of numerous calves. All were black and all looked so much alike to us, it was impossible to distinguish one from another. Yet, in that milling herd every calf knew its (to us) indistinguishable mother, and every cow knew its (to us) indistinguishable calf. To prove this, we made them distinguishable by temporary markings, and separated the calves from the mothers. All found their respective maternal and offspring relationships. Calves left for a while in a particular place at birth are soon found again by the mother, which, so far, does not seem surprising. But let that calf be frightened away from that spot while the mother is absent getting a drink at some distant spring or river and the calf will return to the original spot where it was left for final reunion with its mother, despite the complex route back.

Most of the calves we saw yesterday had been born during the night or in the morning. By afternoon, already capable of mobility, they were herded two miles from the corral to open pasture. (Try to imagine a human being hiking two miles a dozen hours after birth.) The trail led over rough ground and finally crossed the Pecos River. These calves, unfamiliar with water, waded across the river as though having done it through long practice. There was no hesitancy at the brink.

One of the calves was a straggler over the two-mile trail. In fact, it had originally been lying down in a corral and seemed reluctant to rise and follow the herd. We set it on its feet several times and finally decided to determine what would happen if we kept the mother traveling with the herd and left the calf behind. The "indistinguishable" mother soon bolted out of the herd and went back to her (to us) indistinguishable calf. After a few caressing nudges, the calf followed her. We wondered what she had said to the calf in bovine vernacular. The little calf continued to hang back and always the mother returned for it. Finally, after crossing the Pecos River, the mother and calf separated from the herd and were seen off on the range, the calf contentedly nursing.

Call it instinct or miracle. A calf born in the morning actually running, even frolicking, beside its mother by afternoon astounds one.

In a few weeks the calf will begin nibbling grasses to supplement its milk diet. One might draw a moment of delight watching that first nibble of vegetation and do it with an awesomeness over the strange process of nature sustaining her progeny.

The communal spirit in the ranch country rides high when the time comes for rounding up the calves for branding. In spite of the two years of employment on a Montana cattle ranch between the ages of 16 and 18, I cannot wholly adjust to the grim reality of necessary torture that is involved in the preparation of cattle for their growing up on the range. One might avoid the process, but my wife and I get involved in it as inadvertently as if it were custom—she making enormous lunches, I sharpening knives and performing other incidental tasks. The calves get herded into a pen or corral in substantial numbers at a time, where young cowboys who love to test their roping and wrestling ability will, as they pounce on the victimized calf, reach under him for the far front leg to complete

My wife and I get involved in ranch life as inadvertently as if it were custom.

His tender skin is then seared with the branding iron until a cloud of smoke rises.

tripping the animal and throwing him on his side. His tender young skin is then seared with the hot branding iron until a cloud of smoke rises and the air is filled with the smell of burning hair and flesh. Usually, this has to be repeated to complete the whole brand, such as our neighbor's the J-/X, or similar brands. In the meantime one reads hysteria, fright and agonizing pain in the eyes of the prostrate calf, which roars in agony. One might suppose that a badly seared hide is enough torture for this day, but the ordeal is not over.

Castration is the next operation with no surgical niceties of scalpel and anaesthetic. With a cattleman's pocketknife alone the job is done, the calf again bawling in agony. Some cattlemen have a special kind of feast after the roundup, preparing the testicles in a tasty dish, called mountain oysters.

Branded, castrated, dehorned, vaccinated and sprayed, he is now a potential beef steer.

When this might seem the limit of commercial abuse for one day, a dehorning tool is applied. Blood from the sensitive base of each amputated horn runs down over the head of the calf in a gory-clotted mess.

Vaccines and spray wind up the program. The calf, miserable and rhythmically shaking his head in pain, is now a full-fledged, potential beef steer, providing he survives the shock of his ordeal and resists infections in his open wounds. In a couple of weeks he will seem to have forgotten what happened to him, except that when he is fed a supplement, he comes into the feeding area and in apparent recollection he shies away from the cattle pen.

The whole process might seem needlessly cruel. But cattlemen have considered every other possibility that might make the preparation less painful for the critter and easier for the cattlemen. With a large herd the

The time will come when the steers are trucked off to feeding pens.

work must proceed rapidly and economically. Cattle thieves would too easily alter most other tried identification markings. Even the brand burned into the hide of a steer has on occasion been altered, though the compound brands, difficult to change, tend to discourage this.

The time will come when the mature steers are trucked off to feeding pens, then to a packing plant, where eventually they show up in the neat, refrigerated counters of the supermarket as "select cuts," giving no hint to the housewife what the history of these roasts, steaks, and hamburger entails. In packing plants there is no waste. As we often have heard, only the "Moo" has no commercial value.

Those who see life on a ranch for the first time or two, naturally reflect on man's intrepidity in supplying his needs. Man takes life without stint, suffering no apparent remorse or qualms. In fact, he has romanti-

How remarkably the quarter horse falls in with the game.

cized even the grim reality which becomes conventionally and commercially necessary. The young lads who rope and wrestle down the calves for the various operations, do it with a great deal of fun. When the calf roars in agonizing pain it seems only to heighten the sport, where roar and laughter blend in concert.

How remarkably the quarter horse used in the roping, falls in with the game. He knows exactly what to do. As a calf takes off with great speed, the quarter horse, with his rider, is after him with incredible pursuit. As the lariat sails through the air and drops over the calf's neck, simultaneously the quarter horse slams on the brakes, braces himself while the cowboy leaps from the saddle, runs to the calf, reaches for his leg to throw him, and with a few quick loops has the calf bound for branding, castrating, dehorning and incidental treatment. Note in the accompanying illustration how the quarter horse stands with the rope taut, holding, while the cowboy reaches the calf.

No matter what the region of the world or whatever the activity, we shall always be confronted with its dual aspect: the actual and the legendary, the true and the fictional. Perhaps, the actual is too prosaic, too work-a-day, even too grimly real at times to supply the romance needed for general interest. The cowboy does not escape being fictionally a different entity from what he actually is. A reckless group of mounted cowboys, riding through a cow town, six-guns blazing into the air, is perhaps typical of the legendary cowboy visioned by the majority. No specialized group have thus been more unfaithfully represented.

The cowboy as I saw him in Montana near the early part of the 20th century and with whom I lived for two years in bunk house and ranch house was an entirely different human being from the legendary characterization of him, featured in TV scenarios and press, though no less romantic. Here in New Mexico more than a half century later, I find, his equipment is altered but his approach to the raising of beef and his off-range conduct little different.

Strangely, the real, more accurate depiction of the cowboy draws a certain amount of resentment from the general public. It prefers that he exist as the "rootin-tootin-shootin-sonofagun" who will fit into perverted entertainment scenarios. When I suggested, for example, in a film lecture some time ago that timber wolves do not attack human beings, and apparently never have, the audience became blanketed in a kind of disappointing gloom. Cowboys must, thus, fictionally shoot it out with one another in every cow town, or they do not fit into the much-desired, pseudo-traditional life of the West.

To know the West, and to have known the West, is, of course, to know that this daily gun play is mere dramatic humbug. Under the wide-brimmed hat of the cowboy was a human being, subject to all of the emotions, mental and physical reactions peculiar to human beings in other walks of life. That he developed a demeanor, a set of reflexes, and a certain physiological identity from his adjustment to the wilderness range, goes without saying, but it is not an adjustment altering the fact that in the

The cowboy developed a natural identity with the open range.

To best understand the cowboy, one needs to watch him around horses.

majority of his kind, he was and is a generous, tolerant, compassionate human being who can be depended upon to give you a helping hand.

To best understand this description of him, one needs to watch him around horses. In breaking them, he encounters more downright opposition than he is apt to meet in dealing with obstreperous human beings. He has almost the kind of "bedside manner" with horses that a psychiatrist might practice with people in a mental hospital. No matter how utterly perverse the unbroken horse happens to be, the cowboy looks with a certain amusement and tolerance on the horse's every violent protest. He seems to say to his potential mount, "Go ahead and cry it out, you will feel better about it." The cowboy does not fight the animal but avoids its desperation as a woodsman would stand aside to avoid the crash of a felled tree.

But not quite. There comes a time after the horse has been halter, bridle and saddle broken, when the cowboy must wage a contest with the horse, which would much rather be free on the open range than be submissive to the will of man. I suppose that if there could be an understanding between horse and man, the problem of breaking would be almost resolved. But there must be something terribly alien and frightening to a horse in having another creature drape itself around him, not knowing the purpose. The horse probably sees treachery, even extinction, in the act. The final test now comes whether a rider can stay "aboard" when the horse puts his head between his front legs and after leaving the ground a few feet, comes down on all fours, where the rider encounters a jolt of about 5 G's. Or whether the rider can avoid a dozen other unforeseen tricks of violent protest which the bronc conjures up from one moment to the next. Perhaps, the meeting of minds between horse and man begins when, and if, rider and horse are still cohering as one animated mass, and the horse finds as weariness approaches that the creature wrapped around him has, after all, no treacherous intent. About this time the kind and soothing words of the rider may suggest to his mount that no harm was intended. At this stage a horse, if he is not of the outlaw nature, may walk off with his rider comfortably ensconced in the saddle and never again resort to violence.

But with horses as with people, there seems to be a wide difference in temperament, and with a little rest and regeneration of energy, violence may again be resumed. Horses who seem to be well broken may continue their amicable attitudes months, or even years, and apparently from no provocation, go into a sudden rebellion again. As a Missouri mule driver said, "Some mules and horses are like some people, they will be nice to you for ten years in order to give you one swift kick at an opportune moment."

If I have given the impression that the cowboy was always a sanctimonious breed of human being, I must rush to correct this notion. He was on occasion in those much earlier days of the open range, perhaps more rough than fastidious, more inured to the rugged life that he then had to live. All of which should endear him to us the more, for we have seen what fastidiousness, sophistication, sensitivity and the soft life can do to a large share of our present population.

The cowboy's free, bold spirit limited in bygone days only by the blue horizon, his environment in canyon and atop mesa, over billowy prairie, from desert to mountain snow line—these shaped him and tempered him, made him sufficiently indigenous to remain on the range as his only way of life.

His life was and still can be lonely. Gregarious as we all are, he too must seek solace, or rejuvenation, as the case may be. After weeks or months on the range it is not beyond his province to seek the city or the small town for some kind of celebration. I have known trappers whose winter catch was spent in a week or two in a Canadian town, indulging in every sensuality available to them. The cowboy arriving in town for the same diversion implies nothing beyond the social tendencies and needs of all human beings.

Many a young man has, as I did in my earlier days, looked with eager eyes and avid zeal on the possibility of being a cowboy. Riding a spirited horse and possessing all the trappings from lariat to six-gun, had an image that floated daily across my vision, as it does of boys everywhere. The cinema had even attracted young men to America to be cowboys. To most youth it seemed to be a life that left nothing to be desired.

Yet, there is no vocation, I found, that so quickly weeds out the misguided idealist, the weakling, the visionary, and the incorrigible. The illusion of bronco, lariat and six-gun, framed by a wilderness of adventure and leisure, is soon dimmed by days of grueling labor, exposure and a relentless succession of duty that seems to offer none of the romance depicted in the scenario, the pulp stories, and even the classical accounts of the West which have bypassed no less in their realistic treatment much of the dreary aspects of range day labor.

The situation is little different today where the basic aspects of raising beef are concerned. There is much hard work as usual, though every effort has been made to facilitate the various tasks. One no longer packs salt blocks on horses for the long treks to distant grazing areas. Now they are loaded on the pickup or jeep and distributed over the range in a few hours. Supplementary feed that looks like sticks of dynamite, containing special bovine vitamins, minerals and antibiotics, likewise is distributed, along with baled hay. Herds become accustomed to the blast of a horn on the pickup and a little wait will see them in long, meandering, single files coming along trails through canyon and over mesa to be fed.

When we first modernized our *adobe* house, the long, annual absences necessitated installation of an alarm system to thwart break-ins. We considered that the most disturbing sound would be a siren, associating it with the warning of police and fire vehicles. Upon testing it for distance audibility, where we might get cooperation from outlying neighbors in reporting a break-in to the sheriff, we found ourselves surrounded in about half an hour by cattle. The mystery was soon cleared up when we learned that many sirens were installed in pickups to call cattle from the range for supplementary feeding. We later substituted gongs, which we found did not start the salivary glands flowing in the mouths of surrounding range herds.

The pickup, jeep and car have made life a lot less lonely, of course, for the cowboy. He can now make the quick run into town or back to the ranch buildings for meals and lodging from some distant range area. Cattle drives no longer call for weeks on dusty trails. Cattle are trucked to market, or to feeding pens.

We have become as attached to the saddle horse as he to us.

The troublemaker, the gun fighter of the earlier West was not, however, wholly fiction. But he was not, as a rule, the cowboy. He hung around towns that might offer him booty of one kind or another to maintain subsistence at somebody else's expense. If he involved the working cowboy in a confrontation, it was a matter of the cowboy's defense of pride or, in an extreme instance, defense of life. The fact that most cowboys were capable with the six-gun sometimes crowded them competitively into situations toward which they had no inclination.

The six-gun, as a means of settling a dispute, was obviously a very much overplayed aspect of the West. And it is important to know that it was not six-gun law that "tamed" the West. The fast gun of cinema perversion where just about everyone had to prove himself is a bit of nonsense that makes a half dozen TV hours of "Western Drama" per week a profitable medium for advertisers. The sheriff who was faster than all others did not tame the West. What tamed the West, if it ever needed taming in the sense of a pervading outlawry, which it didn't have, was the advent of law itself. The arrogant individual who entered a saloon and threw his weight around as a bully, finally was simply thrown into jail to serve six months for disorderly conduct. When as a bully he merely undertook to insult someone, he was picked up by the local sheriff for using language to provoke an assault and served thirty days to mend his insolent manner. As it became illegal to carry firearms in town, the alleged fast gun, which was a rare occasion, dwindled only into the modern-day cinema. In short, he conducted himself then as he does today in any community, with a sure bet that if he became too cocky, too insulting, he landed in jail. If he so much as threatened to shoot his way out, he was soon again on a holiday from freedom, usually for such a long time as to make his identity almost forgotten in his community. I repeat, it was law with enforcement and not the six-gun that tamed the West, as it was administration of the law that also tamed East, North and South.

Thus, we are inadvertently drawn into ranch life of what we call our *Double T (TT)*. The saddle horses we use are not our own, but a part of the neighboring spread. We have, however, become as attached to them and they to us, as though we were their owners. They come to our gate and hang their heads lazily over it. What can one do but keep feeding them a tidbit and stroking their rangy necks? A part of this is, however, routine convenience. When we need to saddle them, for example, we don't have to round them up; and when we ride them, they accept us.

CHAPTER EIGHT

The Inscrutable Desert

The desert does not particularly welcome the stranger. So much of its vegetation, its cactus, mesquite, etc., has thorns, that any first, rash approach is held at bay. The newcomer gets an impression that all its growth has thorns. It has been said that even its people have thorns, though with some reservations I contest this last accusation. One does not readily, therefore, embrace the desert. Its secrets well kept do not, as with much of the natural world, invite the casual approach.

In a land that must widely space its plants in order that they shall receive their needed allocation of scarce water to survive, protective measures inherently become survival characteristics. One can thus understand why so many plants of the Southwest have, as it were, their own built-in, protective "barbed wire" fences. Many desert plants, such as the cholla cactus and others, have the facility for storing water during dry periods. Obviously, this stored water would be attacked and the plant destroyed by numerous creatures for the water, were it not protected by thorns—though some creatures, such as the *javelina* (wild pig) and others, manage somehow to avert the thorny barrier and get from various cactuses both food and drink.

I became fascinated by the desert to the degree that I was gradually able to gain its acquaintance and avoid its obstacles, or perhaps more accurately, as it condoned in time my alien intrusion.

The nearby desert village of Puerto de Luna (Portal to the Moon) seemed not too farfetched in its connotation. I might have landed with a space vehicle on the moon and experienced no greater amazement than

Many desert plants, such as the cholla cactus, store water through dry periods. (Note inset: water enters voids during rain; voids close to hold water in drought.)

in facing the surrounding desert. As a Northerner accustomed to dense vegetation-cover from ample rain with highly competitive growth over just about every inch of ground area, the bare earth of the North seen only for short spans in newly plowed fields or excavations, my adjustment to the much-open ground and widely-spaced plant life of the desert was not easy to make. In the desert, nature makes an exception to the adage that she abhors a vacuum. Here the generous vacuous intervals of dirt between growth become essential in plant survival.

My wife and I advanced upon the natural scene in the Southwest as greenhorns, but it was not long before we became dabbling amateur naturalists. Ours was not a scientific approach to nature. We hoped to assimilate only some knowledge of the natural Southwest, not with scientific classification, but with sufficient identification of what might be to us the most interesting flora and fauna, the most intriguing geological aspects.

Rather early in our hikes we came upon the plant commonly called the devil's-claw, sometimes referred to as unicornplant or elephant-tusks. More accurately, I might say, it came upon us. We found that it had attached itself to our rough-out boots by means of the two-curved, prong-like appendages on the seed pod—a most extraordinary natural device for distributing its seeds. It is often seen caught on the fetlocks of animals, having the facility to attach itself functionally as a pair of automatic ice tongs. Could one escape wondering how this ingenious natural device came into design?

If my wife and I needed lessons in adjustment to our desert environment, they were to be read from nature just about everywhere. Take the ocotillo, for example, with its "buggy-whip-like" stalk that quickly sprouts leaves after a shower, loses them during the dry periods, whereupon the green bark takes over the plant's function until another moist period arrives. This crop of leaves may occur several times during the year. What a miracle of adaptation! Or consider others, such as the creosote bush with its "varnished" leaves, a waterproof glaze that prevents moisture-loss by evaporation. The phenomenal aspect of this moisture economy in desert plants, while it cannot help but astound, must provide to most of us a kind of lesson in transcending periods of austerity.

In the desert, nature makes an exception to the notion that she abhors a vacuum.

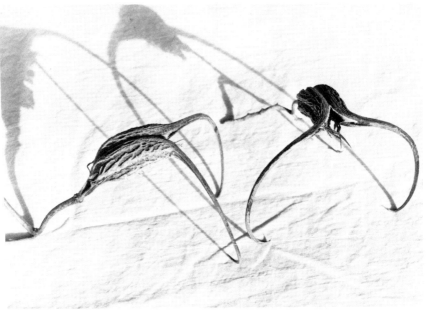

We came upon the plant commonly called the devil's-claw.

Strange enough are even the commoner plants that form seed pods when fully dried, snap open, twist, and fling their seeds for propagation several yards from the parent plant, or the common thistles that send each seed off on an individual parachute. Stranger yet is the heronbill of the Southwest which first twists the seed stem into a tight coil when dry, waits indefinitely for rain, then upon becoming moist, uncoils and literally screws the seed into the ground, utilizing the moist ground germination opportunity. If you have occasion to question the mechanics of this, may I point out that the screw mechanically turns in the right direction for penetration into the ground. These strange propagation devices—can anyone contemplating nature do anything but observe with utter amazement?

If we observe ingenious design in nature and believe that there is nothing insidious about it, what shall we say about the locoweed or jimsonweed that contains a poisonous constituent that causes death to cattle? Loco is a Spanish word that means "crazy," and there we might leave the consideration of this plant.

But consider for a moment being lost on the desert in the early days, dying of thirst and starvation, suddenly seeing hope in the smoke from a campfire in the distance and on reaching it, finding that it is only the smoketree, a gray-green, leafless bush, its plumelike growth creating the astounding illusion of a smoky campfire.

We have compared our seasonal residence in the Southwest with the plant commonly called goldfields, because it actually is not native to the Southwest though it thrives here by a unique cycle of adaptation. It is a plant of the cooler climes and has escaped the heat and drought periods of the Southwest and managed its propagation by a strange off-season adjustment. Like the seasonal resident who has taken advantage of the ideal Southwest climate of winter and spring, so does goldfields (*baeria chrysostoma*) seek an advantage different from plants native to the Southwest. Since goldfields cannot escape the heat and drought to which other plants of the desert have adapted themselves, goldfields passes through the heat and drought period in the dormancy of its seed phase, enjoying bloom during the *winter* rather than the summer periods. The flower is rather small, and in itself not very impressive, but countless blooms suggest a magnificent field of gold.

The ocotillo with its "buggy-whip-like" stalk.

Though goldfields have their beauty in mass, plants in the desert most generally are widely spaced; so, for much the same reason actually, are the people. It was this prospect of a sparse population that intensified my initial interest in the wilds of New Mexico. Many of its other inimitable charms I gradually discovered later.

New Mexico does not have a temperature quite warm enough during the winter months to attract that influx of warmth-seeking humans from the North. If I were to compare New Mexico desert weather with Minnesota, I would say that New Mexico's December-through-February would be comparable to Minnesota's May before the spring growth has emerged. At this moment, February 19, at 2:10 p.m., Mountain Standard Time, the thermometer reads 66° in the shade at our patio. From the sun's warmth I would have guessed 76°. Yet, a week ago snow fell for two and a half days. On the fourth day when the sky cleared, the snow by nightfall had melted and was absorbed into the ground with no runoff. The south wind this afternoon suggests that tomorrow's temperature may reach better than 70°—a temperature that might encourage that warmth-seeking influx of humans from the North to start a New Mexico-bound migration. But these temperature aspirants might also bear in mind before starting south with their eight-cylinder "covered wagons" that a month or more ago the Navajos in the western part of New Mexico were isolated in several feet of snow and had to be assisted with provisions and stock feed dropped from planes.

Yet, under no circumstances would I forego these sudden New Mexico weather changes. They are in a sense another protective inhibitor to insure for us enjoyment of the Pecos Valley and other wild areas with a tolerable degree of wilderness solitude. And if I might suggest a temperature range that is most conducive to comfortable outdoor activity, let it not exceed 70° Fahrenheit. The midwinter temperatures here at this point on the Pecos—indicated by cartographers as on a northern tongue of the Chihuahuan Desert—are usually around 40° when we rise from our early morning beds. By noon it is generally well into the 50s and 60s—on occasion in the 70s.

Night temperatures, as the 40° morning temperature indicates, are consistently cool on the desert. One can crawl with comfort into a down sleeping unit almost any night in a tent camp or open-door cabin.

Poisonous dwellers of the desert are, no doubt, still another factor in maintaining wilderness solitude here on the Pecos. With minor exceptions, north of latitude 45, one has little need to consider poisonous creatures. It isn't necessary in the North as it is in the Southwest, for example, for us to shake out our boots in the morning of an overnight camp to make sure they do not contain a scorpion, or be concerned that in dense growth or rock crevice a rattlesnake will strike from obscurity. Yet, the fears which some Northerners have for such creatures in their Southwest travels are, by long-time experience of native people and our own, we found, obviously magnified beyond need. The hazards are generally classified in about the following manner:

Most of the centipedes are quite harmless. The giant desert centipede, which reaches a length of 6 to 8 inches, can cause a painful inconvenience.

Nor are all scorpions deadly. The yellow, slender-tailed species can be deadly, but usually only to children under four years of age.

The black widow spider, readily identified by the hourglass figure on its belly, is dangerous to man, but now with its wide dispersal—if this is any consolation—can be found in any part of the United States and some parts of Canada. Most of the black widow spider bites clear up in a few days, though some have caused death.

The tarantula—an exaggerated hazard in gruesome tales of fiction, perhaps because of its hoary appearance—scarcely ever bites a human being, and when it does, the bite is usually not serious.

The rattlesnake with which I had much contact in my earlier days in Montana, is the most feared perhaps of the poisonous desert dwellers. He knows that his lack of speed hampers his escape facility. While he tries to be innocuous by stealthily crawling away, he will, if pursued or cornered, strike out. His rattle is usually warning enough to avoid him, though not always. He is abroad especially in the summer night—a fact too often overlooked—and may lie across your path. We found that a flashlight is quite indispensable even on a moonlit evening. It is commonly believed that the rattlesnake will not cross a rope, especially a hair rope, laid around a camp, but this I have proved is mere fictional fancy. It ranks with the belief that anyone with a rattlesnake skin hatband will be in danger of being struck by lightning.

Generally speaking, common precautions we found make the hazards of poisonous desert dwellers of no special concern. Children, of course, should be watched rather closely. During our winter stay we are oblivious to poisonous dwellers and raise a casual guard only as the rising temperatures in April begin to bring them out.

Appraisal of the desert has generally been made by how man was able to make his adjustment to it. This has been especially evident where early settlement by the white man was concerned. His modern adjustment to it is, of course, apparent. But I think the most significant relationship of man to the desert is derived from the early Indian's relation to it and his survival techniques, both against nature and against the white man who tried to exterminate him for personal gain.

Though one may become eager for knowledge where subject matter is new, and at times awed in the presence of tales indigenous to a strange land, such as our exposure to the Southwest, it is well, I find, not to accept too readily the current concepts which one often has to unlearn later on closer inspection. Henry Ford once said, "History is bunk." While this presumption may be too general to accept whole hog, history, as most of us have observed, is indeed often "bunk."

Perhaps history is particularly "bunk" where many of the records of Indian encounters with the white army in the early settlement of the Southwest desert are concerned. I was especially anxious to examine this phase of our history. History slanted for popular consumption might give us the notion that the Indian was readily and systematically removed from the desert ranch and mountain lands to make room for general settlement. Vast areas still remaining to the Indian as reservations are obvious proof that he was neither readily nor systematically removed. It might be said that the Apache, now ensconced on a substantial portion of his original New Mexican area, as Charles F. Lummis so poignantly revealed, is "laughing to scorn a nation of . . . millions," that had sought to rob and extinguish him.

The Land of Poco Tiempo by Lummis, published in 1893, a classic of early New Mexico, is not a document, we can presume, that conventional historians care to impose upon the tender, self-adulating, reading public of today. The effect it would have on the current Indian problem now so explosive would be too significant in pointing up the Southwest's responsibility.

The Apache learned just enough about civilization to avoid its military follies. Being set upon for complete extermination by the army (a fact shunted aside whatever history is written), the Apache became the most elusive, perhaps the most formidable, individual guerrilla-type of desert warrior the world has known. Being exceptionally few in number compared to the army, the Apache exacted a toll of at least twenty soldiers to the loss of one of his own. Just previous to April 1886, the Apache had killed between three and four hundred of his attackers while losing only two of his own tribe. When the army with its cumbersome equipment rolled over desert range, around mesa and through canyon, confronting the Apache, each warrior—a wholly independent, self-sustaining, fighting unit within himself—vanished behind the rocks with the disappearance of a flushed covey of Gambel's Quail, where the Indian managed to fire almost at will upon the exposed army encumbered by its clumsy gear.

The military—suffering incredible defeat—refused to accept the plea of a particular, saner group of civilians whose compassion for the common soldier and the Indian sought to bring about a compromise in the sharing of the Apache's land which he so rightfully and stubbornly refused to give up. Range exploiters, politicians, and the army ultimately had to learn the hard way. A compromise was finally made that by any sense of human decency could have been achieved without loss of military dignity or the decimation of armies in the first place. In the present day when the killing has ceased, the need for an equitable compromise is no less urgent. The Apache's present reserve lands originally thought to be almost worthless and therefore fit for Indian reservations, fortunately contain rich uranium finds and other valuable resources—a troublesome mote still in the eye of the invidious racist element, and it grows with aggravation each successive day.

The historical standoff that has allowed a large Indian population to survive the army's decimation design, was obviously due to the greatest examples of desert wilderness craft and military survival technique ever manifested by any small ethnic group. It deserves here some narrating at the risk of deviating from our overall theme as greenhorns, though every aspect of life touches the initiate who finds residence in the Southwest.

In the main the Apache understood and practiced one factor of warfare which has troubled armies and wilderness expeditions since the beginning of history—*mobility*.

Mobility the Apache understood all too well and used to his advantage. Like a swarm of elusive hornets they would buzz unseen around the cumbersome, pursuing white army with its harness mules and camp gear, "sting" many of the soldiers to death, then rapidly disappear.

As the army lost its men through massacre and its horses through stampede, the Apache acquired the animals for his own maneuvers. But the horses were not, as by the army, used for permanent mounts. When army reinforcements were brought up to pursue the warriors, the Apache deliberately rode the captured army horses until they dropped from exhaustion, slashed their throats and lived on "pony steaks" or had a mescal roast while the army lumbered along with its heavy equipment in ineffectual pursuit.

Water from desert springs and from the sky determined much of the military strategy. The Apache needed, of course, to carry water as well as the army, but the Apache resorted to no such hazardous method as the hauling of water barrels. Instead, he drew and cleansed the large intestine from the army horses which he had ridden to death, wound them around the bodies of live mounts, filled the intestines with water, and then disrupted the spring's flow upon leaving, so it would not be of immediate use to the army. The water-carrying horses could then move with the speed of the Indian warriors' mounts. This rapid mobility gave the Apache warrior days of respite far ahead of the army, when he could rest, enjoy a mescal roast and other substantial food.

We need only cast our vision across an expanse of the apparently austere New Mexico desert to make us wonder how the Apache managed from the desert's limited flora and fauna to extract his provisional needs. The austere appearance of the desert is one thing, the actual affluent substance becomes quite something else.

It was, for example, the young bud stalks from the mescal (agave or century plant) that the Apache used for his much-desired roasts. When the Apache had gained, by his superior mobility, enough time over his pursuing enemy, he dug a pit, lined it with rock; and from greasewood, cedar, piñon pine and mesquite roots, as they circumstantially and variously afforded his firewood, he kept a fire going in the pit until it was baking hot. On the hot stones in the pit he laid a layer of grass, then mescal shoots, another layer of grass, another layer of mescal, etc., until the pit was filled. The whole prepared roast was then laid over with a topping of grass, hot rocks, and finally dirt, to bake from two to four days.

For these cooking periods no fire existed to emit smoke and betray the Apache's position, yet preparation of the feast was nevertheless going on. Through the dirt covering were left protruding a few of the bayonet-shaped leaves of the agave plant. When the mescal roast was considered done, one of these leaves was pulled. If it was done at the tip where it penetrated into the roasting mescal, the pit was opened and the feast began. If not, another leaf was later pulled and still later another until the "proof of the pudding was in the eating."

Since the roasted mescal would keep for several months, the size of the roast even during oppressive times became rather large. On the warpath the Apache simply ate his fill and was gone. The army, coming upon the Apache's camp, expecting an engagement, found only empty mescal pits. Sometimes one or more of the full mescal pits were still there when the army arrived, well covered and camouflaged, the army's attention diverted by simulated, empty mescal pits.

Another food available to the Apache was the ripe beans of the mesquite, ground to flour (pinole) in the metate with a mono (millstone and hand-size boulder). The heavy metates, not carried, were cached in many a convenient hiding place or merely turned upside down to resemble only a native stone. One finds them today around ruins or on the sites of early Indian campgrounds, many having been carried off to museums or to someone's home as artifacts. The Southwest has many of these metates gracing domestic flower and rock gardens.

Fruit from the Spanish bayonet, dried in the sun, seeds from the piñon pine (now even sold commercially), and mountain acorns, are only a few of the wild foods the Apache had available to him the length and breadth of the desert and mountains. Antelope, deer, turkey, fish, rabbit, along with range cattle and sheep (the domestic source from open ranch herds to which the Apache generously helped himself) made the cumbersomeness of carrying food supplies over desert and mountain quite needless, as he fought off his military pursuers.

Commercially, today, meat from the rattlesnake, locust, and many heretofore seemingly unpalatable foods, have become a special epicurean delicacy, sold in exclusive food shops and featured on the menus of high-ranking restaurants. The Apache was aware of these foods and it was this knowledge and their wide availability that made him such a master of his desert environment. He was not even averse, as Lummis pointed out, to routing with a stick a number of field mice from the matted leaves lodged in the base of a mesquite bush and roasting them. We cannot say that our appetites are less fastidious than his, for we have only been deceived by the apathies of squeamish people who did not know dietary possibilities and often starved to death in a land of plenty.

CHAPTER NINE

New Mexican Wilderness Culture

It is self-evident that as my wife and I took up seasonal residence in the Southwest, we would be intrigued by its culture, especially since New Mexico perhaps has one of the most focused upon art areas on the continent. The focus being largely upon the wilderness culture of the Southwest, it became even more intriguing. We were, therefore, anxious to examine as best we could, what lay behind this great concentration of art upon the wilderness.

Most of us tend to regard some particular area on earth as greater in beauty and interest than all others. This might be attributed to high aesthetic appreciation but, no doubt, is a form of nostalgia based on living in a certain locality for a long time or being in some region through circumstance where by virtue of the advantages which appealed to us, we have decided to make our home. But when we consider New Mexico, it seems that we need to regard it objectively rather than with sentimental or provincial standards of judgment. New Mexico has so forcefully drawn the artist from various parts of the world, one is tempted to judge New Mexico's beauty and wilderness culture more as to how it might appear from a broad, cosmopolitan derived viewpoint.

D. H. Lawrence, for example, said ". . . for greatness of beauty I have never experienced anything like New Mexico." Even after my wife and I had accepted the fact that here lies beauty, wild and incomparable, we were anxious to search further for some obscure reason why New Mexico's attraction for the artist has been so overwhelming.

The beginning of the artist influx, according to early and late biographers and historians, seems to have centered on a rather simple though highly significant event that took place in 1896. Frederick Remington, perhaps the most dramatic of artists painting the West, had, of course, visited here before 1896, making sketching trips in the 1880s and working up these sketches in 1902. But we find well documented that the artist, Joseph Sharp, had been in the region and vividly described it to another artist, Ernest L. Blumenschein, who became intrigued by Sharp's inspiring account. As winter was approaching, Blumenschein and Bert Greer Phillips bought a wagon and team of horses in Denver, for the purpose of working their way down into Old Mexico, planning apparently to move along with the sun's southward declination.

Roads then were rough, mere ruts on the softer ground and scarcely discernible over whatever rocky terrain that permitted any kind of wagon passage. Blumenschein and Phillips, according to their biographers, had not been accustomed to handling horse-drawn equipment over such uncertain, hazardous routes. Consequently, in northern New Mexico near the San Luis Valley their wagon, while not collapsing like the "One Hoss Shay," did break down. They needed the repair of a damaged wheel and Blumenschein's side of a flipped coin chose him to make the trip, converting one of their harness horses into a mount. Taos happened to be situated along their scheduled route. Blumenschein, on arriving in Taos, became entranced by the region, seeing in the Pueblo Indian culture and the fantastically beautiful mountain scenery infinite subject matter. Integrally, the environment was fresh, challenging, naturalistically compelling, and profoundly satisfying to the artist eye.

Phillips, too, caught the mood of Blumenschein's enthusiasm and both decided to settle in Taos. Later, Blumenschein again met Sharp, and soon thereafter, met E. Irving Couse who was convinced by the description given by them that Taos had extraordinary advantages for the artist.

By 1915 the artist influx to Taos had snowballed, until over a hundred artists had by then arrived. This it seems was partly due to The Taos Society Traveling Exhibition. But the air of Taos had already become electrified by the earlier artist influence. Also, visitor and settler alike, who had enjoyed the wildly beautiful country, the pueblo culture, and the edifying cultural atmosphere created by artists, gave voice to these values whenever they went to the outside for a visit.

Santa Fe, as well, with the same general attributes of mountain grandeur and Pueblo Indian culture, was also beginning to enjoy its own developing art colony. Here, it seems, Carlos Vierra was the first artist to make Santa Fe his home.

What essentially, we asked, were the elements that, by contrast with the rest of the nation, made New Mexico such an irresistible center of concentration for artists? We can assume that much of the United States, even early in the century, was becoming more and more stereotyped by agrarian and industrial development. The artist, consequently, moved about looking for that which did not obtrude conventionally or monotonously upon his artistic eye. He went to Europe when he became frustrated in his search for the unusual, only to find that myriad artists had preceded him, painting to repletion the subjects that had the Old Country archaic charm. Be this as it may, I am inclined to believe that it was the unusual nature of the pueblo culture, complemented by the unique mountain setting of these pueblos, still further complemented by the mild climate which allowed almost year-round outdoor painting, that in toto lay at the bottom of the artist's lure, and gave him so much artistic satisfaction. But we must not overlook the rapprochement between artists which manifested itself so admirably in this region, the high communal spirit that seems stronger among artists than any other group. Taos and Santa Fe now have those intimate coffee shops which we found such delightful meeting places for cultural interrelationships. Even the nonartist, sophisticated tourist patronizing these places, finds himself in an aura of cultural enjoyment—a feeling of having escaped the prosaic business and industrial world for the interval and enjoying a kind of intellectual ennoblement.

From the artist-interest standpoint in New Mexico, we also should not overlook the emergence over several centuries of an amalgamated Indian, Mexican, Spanish culture deeply rooted in the natural environment. The shelters of these people, in the majority, were primitive and picturesque, largely of *adobe* and native stone with *adobe* mortar. Floors, as I have indicated elsewhere, were often of dirt, hardened by mixing ox blood with the caliche soil. It was a culture little disturbed by the stereotype of Anglo-American money-hardened influence. The artist influx was, of course, mostly "Anglo," but the general population was not Anglo, thus holding back for some time the industrial Anglo routing of the native culture.

As time went on, the overriding stereotype that had swept most of the country began to intrude upon the true tempo of the leisure artist, losing for him much of his early serenity and pristine subject matter. With the rapid influx of industry, he started to paint under stress, hoping to depict what the culture of the area held before it became too industrially prosaic.

Even as late as 1883, however, Sharp was surprised to discover that the Indians still lived in a somewhat natural state, and he became anxious to paint the true Indian life before it vanished.

Frederick Remington on his arrival in New Mexico, said:

"The Americans have gashed this country up so horribly with their axes, hammers, scrapers and plows that I always like to see a place which they have overlooked; some place before they arrive with their heavy-handed God of Progress."

We might, therefore, think of the Taos and Santa Fe regions as enjoying for fifty years a kind of naturalistic renaissance from 1882 on to 1932, a period before the "heavy-handed God of Progress" rode rough-shod into New Mexico to "improve" out of existence the priceless earlier natural advantages to the artist.

Today, when the artist paints the Pueblo Indian, he paints him more as he used to be, using whatever genuine props he can buy or borrow from the salvaged culture of the past. Something irretrievable has obviously been lost. Galleries now line the streets of Taos and Santa Fe, but we found that the paintings which art collectors appear to seek most are those which came to life early in Taos and Santa Fe art history, when the Pueblo Indian culture was still vibrantly alive and undisturbed, the wilderness areas still inviolate.

The modern-day method of purchasing a great painting is almost routine. An art collector arrives and learns that somebody owns one of the early paintings which likely no longer hangs in a local gallery. A local or long distance phone call is made to its owner to learn its availability and its latest time-escalated price. The early artist, lying beneath the red

This illustration of the roadrunner typifies what I am trying to say.

soil of New Mexico, or elsewhere, were he alive today, would, no doubt, be astounded by the growing high appreciation and monetary value of his work. But he, more than anyone else, would know that it was not only the result of his ingenious brush, but also that it was integrally a product of the great naturalistic era in which he worked.

Despite the feeling of nostalgia for the early art of the Southwest, not for a moment do I want to suggest that the painter's art is diminishing. It has changed as, of course, all of life has changed. If space in this short chapter permitted, one might want to dwell enthusiastically on the work that is being done today, especially on the artists themselves, for it is the colonial spirit of the Southwestern graphic art colonies that, I believe, has no parallel among its groups on earth.

One would avidly pose those artists, of course, who have impressed one more uniquely than others—especially those perhaps who have become more indigenous to the Southwest environment which shapes their art, and which, in turn, so much shapes the whole Southwest cultural attitude.

Perhaps the most novel work in Southwest wilderness culture we have seen is that done by Jack Drake of Carlsbad, New Mexico. The accompanying illustration of the roadrunner typifies what I am trying to say. One might conclude from an observation of the photo that photographic ingenuity had provided an unusually fine camera shot, or that an artist in oils had succeeded most admirably in depicting this extraordinary member of the cuckoo family. It is neither. It is, in fact, though incredible, a wood carving of both roadrunner and lizard, with a fidelity of expression that eludes even the most critical. Jack Drake has been dubbed an "Audubon in Wood," and we might question if Audubon succeeded in painting his shot-and-stuffed birds with more reality than those carved from wood by Jack Drake.

The roadrunner, New Mexico's state bird, has raced across our yard almost daily. Yet, all the raw chicken eggs, hamburger, and other delicacies we have offered him as inducements to pause long enough for a photo have been lost in poor timing. When blinds and camera are set, he does not come. When we are busy with other things, he cunningly gobbles our bait and is gone. We might have returned to the North without a photo of this delightful creature, had not Jack Drake come to our rescue with a photo of his carving. I can vouch that Jack Drake's roadrunner appears in the photo as an exact replica of the one which makes those fleeting sojourns through our yard. No less, the Southwest birds on the whole which he reproduces in wood, appear to be exact replicas of those I see through my field glasses.

As one visits Taos, Santa Fe, and other points to observe early Indian culture in New Mexico, one sees it suffering a serious conflict with modern trends.

It may seem strange, and perhaps it is the political paradox of all times, that the Pueblo Indian governors should go en masse to Washington, as they did, for the sole purpose of *preventing* the inclusion of their people in civil rights legislation. But when we examine such legislation where it concerns the Pueblo Indian culture, we find that the legislation is not written on a basis of live and let live for the Pueblo Indian, or to allow him his self-determination. Inadvertently, or perhaps intentionally, it casts aside the tribal laws that effectually governed the Pueblo Indian for thousands of years, and involves him in a complex and arbitrary set of costly legal processes which muddle up his life and impose on him a system of legal concepts he cannot afford or apply practically to his advantage. (It is inconceivable to a vast population, caught in the confining industrial obsessionism, that the Indian has a right not to be victimized by this commercial chaos that is threatening the viability of all living things. No matter what our lifestyle, the Indian has a right to his own.)

In the Pueblo judicial system when something is stolen, as for example, a sheep, and the thief is found out, he is not subjected to white man's punitive measures, such as the public support of a costly prison sentence, but is required to return the stolen sheep and nine more, or their equivalent in labor, to his victim. This may seem like a rather odd form of judicial procedure. Yet, in its direct simplicity and compensatory value lies the secret. The Pueblo Indian thus has avoided complication of his problems. We might consider that modern man with his infinitely complex and arbitrary legal processes could similarly utilize simple directives derived from this example. Long before Thoreau suggested it, the Pueblo Indian was doing his "bookkeeping on a thumbnail."

We need have no illusions. The Pueblo Indian is bound to be in continual conflict with the incursion of legislative and industrial "progress" that eventually will pass indiscriminately over him, as it has over all other racial minority naturalistic cultures. The incursion might better be described as the monolithic stone that rolls over too many priceless values and cultures in order that whatever emerges afterward should categorically and indisputably according to convention, be placed in the undifferentiated, solid uniformity of society, based primarily on commercial value.

While the pueblo culture will eventually be reduced to a mere record by conventional inroads, we can at least preserve the pueblo structures themselves as monuments, along with numerous Indian artifacts, the literary and painted depictions, and the oral or documentary expressions from the Indian descendants themselves. With the recent demand by various ethnic groups for an historical place in the sun, Pueblo Indians may be the most outstanding traditionalists for the preservation of their forebears' knowledge and the early shape of life.

Of these to set the pace are a number of Taos Indians, presently occupying the area. Some are magnificently aged who retain a great deal of firsthand knowledge of the past; others, young adults, handsome, athletic in build, racially fit subjects for the brush of the most accomplished artist. Taos Indian craft shops are in operation at this time, one especially significant that stocks items manufactured by the present Pueblo Indians themselves. While I visited this shop a Pueblo Indian brought in several sets of bows and arrows for tourist sale, made from natural materials gathered in the surrounding mountain area.

My opportunities over more than a half century to observe various North American Indians, always bring home to me a salient factor: what might be termed the inherent natural skill of these people. In the Indian craft shop I tried to watch unobtrusively a young Indian lad—surely less than eight years of age—kindling a fire in a *fogón,* the *adobe* fireplace typical of the Southwest. The deftness with which he handled a sharp belt knife to create readily flammable feathersticks and splintered wood on which the fire would climb, obviously was learned from his parents of long experienced fire building, but I refused to leave this without thinking that generations of such fire building dexterity inherently controlled in part the reflexes in those little hands. As the smoke rose in the chimney, I walked over to the fireplace to catch the fragrance of burning piñon pine and feel a bit of warmth in the coolness of the morning. I would not dare say whether the fire or that youngster's eyes glowed with more inspiration as he saw me take advantage of his achievement.

On a wall hung a framed certificate from the United States Department of the Interior, Indian Arts and Crafts, honoring the owner of the Indian craft shop for work in this field. His dealings with tourist customers manifested a practical life's experience, a captivating naturalistic philosophy.

Indians from the Pueblo came to loiter and visit. We talked about down-to-earth, elemental aspects of the wilderness. Said one, "If the tourist would only stop long enough to blink his eyes once in a while as he passes through, he might see the wonders and grandeur of Nature. I feel sorry for the kids. Parents should do something for the kids if not for themselves." The owner's interest lay close to the wilderness, yet it carried the sophistication of one long in contact with world affairs.

His wife thought it strange that in her trip to Canada's EXPO 67, she did not see any Indians—the Ojibway and Cree—something she had looked forward to enjoying. As I explained to her, with Canada's large and widely dispersed Indian population, this failure to see Indians was more a coincidence than a normal condition.

In the Indian craft shop, besides current trade items, were many rare artifacts—heirlooms gathered from the Taos Pueblo early culture. It might seem that anyone with a well-filled purse could gather here mementos of the early Indian craft and culture of New Mexico. But while there was an excellent stock of late Indian-crafted items, those of early pueblo life were not for sale. With a note of apology came the inevitable answer to a bid for purchase, "I am saving them for my kids. I want them to know that they are the direct descendants of the Taos Pueblo people who used these very items. They can then pass them down to their own kids." And to this one could only reply that wisdom and sentiment ride high in the saddle.

No matter how we regard the pueblo culture of today and its dissolution in the conventional tomorrow, we will still have at least the material and documentary components to reconstruct in our minds the pueblo culture as it existed before the wheels of agricultural and industrial development rolled relentlessly westward. With my more than half a century of living close to the wilderness, it is not difficult, I feel, to turn back time with the materials and knowledge at hand and conjure up what pueblo life to a large extent might have been like in its pristine state.

This may seem a bit presumptuous coming from one who has lived in New Mexico only part time for seven years. Yet, as I see the existing artifacts and having had considerable contact with the basic essentials of wilderness life and natives elsewhere, I find New Mexican Indian life if not in utilitarian detail, then basically the same from the north to the south tip of the continent. Since we are all human prototypes, it is very likely that a Pueblo Indian would adjust as quickly to the wilderness life I have come to know in Canada, as I, a Caucasian, in the short span of seven years, have in a measure adjusted to the Chihuahuan Desert and the Sangre de Cristos of the Rocky Mountains where the Pueblo and other Indian tribes live.

One does not feel comfortable about invading the privacy of the pueblo people, who are averse to the intrusion, but I was made welcome after a respectful explanation of my purpose. My desire to record briefly some aspects of the pueblo life was readily sanctioned, although some of them thought, and rightly so, that a Pueblo Indian would be best equipped to do it.

There arises an illusion here. I was as expectant by what I hoped to see as the reader will be who anticipates herein a description of pristine living in an Indian pueblo. That is long gone. The pueblo interiors I visited had already lost their original appointments. I can best ask the reader to enter the living quarters of a low-income dwelling to learn what most pueblo interiors are like at this time. Need one without anguish say more?

Obviously, man as archetype is not far removed from man in any ethnic culture, race or society, a point of immense importance, I think, in evaluating humanity anywhere. The life my wife and I live within the modernized *adobe* walls of our cabin on the Pecos River of New Mexico is not essentially different except in the degree of modernization from that lived by the Indians within the *adobe* walls of a pueblo. All of us, no matter what the race, must have the basic essentials to provide and prepare food, acquire clothing and bedding, maintain social interest, seek amusement, perform physiological functions, and otherwise conduct the daily affairs of life, as all ethnic groups do throughout the world in various degrees of austerity or luxury.

I examined the *hornos* (*adobe* ovens) which baked the earlier pinole bread of the Pueblo Indians and now bake various cereal breads, though today most of it is baked in mail order stoves. The *hornos* perform the task extraordinarily well. I have long known and used earthen ovens in Montana, and appreciated basically the Pueblo Indian's asset here. With the strong bonding element of caliche in the *adobe* soil, the ovens are made like domes, resembling large beehives. In Montana they are dug out of clay banks. In both types a wood fire is burned within the oven until the interior earthen walls are heated to a baking temperature which it holds throughout any extended baking period. The oven is then brushed free of ashes and the bread, meat, or other items placed within to bake from the retained heat. The bread is placed inside and removed with a wooden oven peel. Bread and roasts baked in these ovens are uniformly baked on all sides and for this reason seem to acquire an especially delicious flavor because of the rich-brown overall crust that forms. In fact, a number of commercial bakery ovens still operate to this day on the same basic principle (now preheating a firebrick lining in the oven) because the same flavorful result is somehow not obtainable in gas or electric ovens. (I am not certain whether this is entirely true, and that it is partly due to prejudice or sentiment. I do find in my wilderness cabin in Canada that bread baked in a wood range seems tastier than by gas or electric ovens.)

Wherever one travels in the wilderness areas of New Mexico to observe the Indian culture, two factors, of course, stand predominantly in the foreground of consideration—water supply and existing available food sources. The Taos Pueblo yard area is divided by a mountain stream which has provided the pueblo people with an abundance of food through irrigation. Corn, squash and beans were the early crops raised. Analysis of these three food items will point up their highly balanced nutritional value, particularly their complement value to the meat and fish obtained in the nearby wilderness. Away from the highways, in the wild mountain

The *horno* (baking oven), resembling a large beehive.

regions, one becomes aware of this food supply that must have been a highly sustaining source for the Pueblo Indian and still is to some extent. Elk, deer, bear, and small game, along with fish from mountain streams and lakes, have down through the years been extensively available throughout the mountain region, complementing the Indian's agricultural products. Besides, there were a number of wild foods such as piñon nuts, berries, mescal, and others which further supplemented game and cultivated items. That he lived well and confident in his supply leaves little doubt.

As one considers early Indian life in its more pristine state anywhere over the continent, it becomes evident that nature has been quite generous and varied in providing food, clothing and shelter. In my book, *Paradise Below Zero,* I considered the winter shelters of the Cree Indian, his birchbark tepee, and the Eskimo's early snowhouse. Both the northern Indian and the Eskimo lived seasonally in severe winter climates and not only survived, but maintained a highly viable existence.

Though a large share of Pueblo Indians lived in high altitude mountain temperatures (Taos and Santa Fe being about 7,000 feet) they had the natural assets of *adobe* in their region for providing warm shelters, maintaining a high degree of comfort and livability, giving them a margin in shelter advantage perhaps over northern tribes. The mean mountain temperatures were not as warm through the winter as those enjoyed by pueblo dwellers in the desert below, but they are, nevertheless, fairly mild. *Adobe* being the best even of modern building materials in the Southwest, it provided the Pueblo Indian with more than adequate shelter. *Adobe* also gave him an excellent material for interior fireplace heating. With the surrounding mountains abounding in piñon pine, the most fragrant of all firewoods, he had a purchase on his environment that left little to be desired. (A significant point of Indian culture to consider is that of all materials on earth, substantial shelters can be built with *adobe* without modern tools.)

As we interview and study the pueblo people we realize that down through the ages they had an awareness philosophy not only of their material advantage, but also of the magnitude and scenic beauty in their area. Of this they spoke most heartily. Is it any wonder that even to this day they seek a continued independence from white man's political influence and interference, a deeply inherent passion to be self-determining and self-sustaining?

I got an insight into the wealth of nature in the region which is now Santa Fe, when I discovered that the Indians saw fit to build nine pueblos within a radius of thirty-four miles. Food, clothing, and shelter in a land of wildly extravagant beauty were, perhaps, never more generously bestowed in early times anywhere on earth. A high Indian culture was thus bound to flourish here.

As we traveled into other wilderness areas of the Southwest, we found that pristine Indian survival rested on the same basic premises as elsewhere—the availability of water, food and shelter. But we are awed when these seem to have been meted out in an austere way severely modified from that of the mountain pueblo life.

In a wild mesa and canyon country southeast of the Pecos River where we have our irrigated ranch, I came upon a rockbound arroyo that obviously was the home of early man for countless years. Untold ages of flash rainstorms typical of this area had worn down the rock to form a gorge. The water drop of about thirty feet between two elevations had created a basin in the rock deep enough to store up a substantial, permanent supply of rainwater.

The overhanging rock cornice in the canyon at the pool, had apparently been created by a capillary-attraction, water-erosion process under the overhead rock, providing an excellent, roomy shelter. The surrounding country being a good habitat for deer, antelope—and, no doubt, in those earlier periods, buffalo—made permanent habitation here tenable. The accumulated carbon from ages of fires in front of the cavelike rock overhang gives some hint of the pristine living that went on in this arroyo. In fact, the type of artifacts we found, indicated that life here had gone on from very early periods, when no commercial items were available, on up to white man's incursion: spear and arrowheads of flint buried in stratas below empty cartridge cases. Even a pair of high-button shoes were secreted on an inner secluded shelf of rock, probably owned by some fair Indian maiden less than a century ago.

So far, I have not managed to obtain a radiocarbon or potassium-argon test to determine how long ago human beings made their homes in this arroyo, but I am continually made aware by successive finds here of masterfully-crafted flint tools and pottery shards that these were not some low-sensitivity creatures who grimly put in their years among these rocks, the pool and the surrounding game area, but were undoubtedly people who had much the same intrinsic responses to environmental factors—to beauty, pleasure, rich human relationships, and others that we, their prototypes, experience.

The flint knives, arrowheads, spearheads, skin scrapers, and pottery shards we found in the area of this arroyo, suggest that the people who lived here were primarily hunters. The immediate region is too arid to suppose that any agriculture might have taken place, and the limited water supply and dependence on light rainfall would suggest at once that irrigation was not carried on here as it has been done by the early people in some of the other regions in New Mexico. Irrigation could, of course, have been employed in places remote from their immediate arroyo habitat, along streams several miles away, but there is a greater likelihood that these streams primarily offered fish from the waters and game along the banks.

Also, one must not overlook the wild vegetable foods that were available here—piñon nuts and others mentioned in Chapter Eight. A certain amount of conjecture is required in presuming from observation of artifacts and shelter ruins what New Mexico's earliest culture was. Yet, along the rivers on elevations that might provide a good campground and an observation point for spotting possible enemy incursion, we found much revealing material: numerous flint knappings, some arrowheads, pottery shards, metates (millstones) and monos, the latter being the boulder held in the hand pushed back and forth in the metates to grind the seeds and grain for flour. Beyond these, one can by logical conjecture fill in many antecedent blanks.

How early man came here and what happened to those who abandoned cave and pueblo permanently, now rest on still wider speculation and scientific analysis. Whatever the answers are, I invariably arrive at these places and depart with ever-growing amazement at man's ingenious, early capability of surviving gracefully in the existing natural environment against much adversity, nevertheless, with an apparent wealth of that glad-to-be-alive reaction to each day.

CHAPTER TEN

Anglophobia

To the right and across the irrigation ditch from the doorway of our *adobe* dwelling on the Pecos when we first arrived, stood the *adobe*-mortared stone wall remains of what apparently was a settlement cabin when the land on which it stands was Mexico proper—not what it is now, the state of New Mexico in the United States. This territorial transition might seem of no present-day significance were it not for the residual effect that has lingered since the military conflict between the United States and Mexico.

As we saw the semi-ruins, time had reduced the *vigas,* the door and window frames, and whatever other wood that was used in the construction of this original cabin, to humus, now long lost in the red New Mexican soil. And time would have leveled the present stone walls, too, were it not that the builder by training, or more likely just natural aptitude, laid stone upon stone so symmetrically, made the walls so widely stable, gravity could have little effect in tumbling the walls to the ground.

Just as the walls stood through history, they continued to stand long after we had made fully habitable the principal *adobe* dwelling. While life goes on in the present, we are continually being made aware of what these walls represented of a past—an ethnic culture which impinges on present-day life. We had deposited ourselves in an Hispanic-Mexican-American community, much as a cowbird lays her alien eggs in the nest of another species for incubation and acceptance. While my wife is of German extraction and I of Swedish, we were, nevertheless, regarded as "Anglos." There might not seem to be an ethnic difference here of great moment between the Hispanic population and us, but when I learned that a Chinese, opening a restaurant in a New Mexican town, was also considered an "Anglo," the broad distinction made between native and "intruder" was no longer difficult to comprehend.

One can understand the residual effect of war where hate tends to linger, but the racial prejudice itself which has followed the conflict between the United States and Mexico is little more than depravity. Americans of Mexican ancestry being refused service in restaurants reaches a new low. Violence becomes repugnant where it is mere incorrigible conduct, but I see little need to suffer moral qualms where, in retaliation, violence follows the refusal of restaurant owners to serve people because of their skin color. A former Mexican-American U. S. Army soldier whose home was in New Mexico and who was refused food in a Texas restaurant, is a cardinal example of this social corruption. Hungry, he waited on and on while all in the restaurant were served. When finally he asked for service, the owner said, "We are closing." Soon thereafter several customers came in and were served. The recourse here should have been that the establishment be padlocked until the owner was prosecuted, sentenced or heavily fined. The chances are, of course, that this soldier would have gotten nowhere in a legal complaint. When the soldier insisted upon being served and finally was told, "We don't serve Mexicans in here," there was but one recourse, and it happened. Fellow soldiers entered the restaurant, smashed up the fixtures and beat up the proprietor. Conveniently, the regiment was shipped out and the matter died—a form of military field strategy that deserves commendation.

But such acts of racial bigotry are not easily forgotten. They smolder long after in cold wars. "Gringo" and "Wasp" (White Anglo Saxon Protestants) are terms that linger on one side, while "Wetbacks" and "Greasers" linger on the other, to denounce racially. Intelligent populations of both races do everything in their power to create an amicable situation, and I must agree that it is a growing success. There seems to have been more progress racially in the past five years than we have seen in the previous hundred. Strict legislation along with a pride by every ethnic group that results in violence whenever persecution takes place, may eventually be the correcting forces that will reduce racial prejudice to an insignificant minimum.

That wars do not wholly settle boundaries and differences in political, ideological or religious concepts, should be apparent by now to everyone. But the fact that boundaries do inevitably change from time to time by military force, by diplomatic skirmish and other means, and have so changed throughout man's historical recollection, would show that man must inevitably go on living with as little conflict as possible in the disputed areas, otherwise he does not prosper but merely suffers the kind of internal erosion which eventually destroys him.

Few nations, if history tells, come into being with clean slates; most are invaders. The invaded more than likely have an earlier history that might best for diplomatic advantage be relegated to the lost limbo of the past. Boundary disputes rest on so many ramified factors, those who hope to establish a position of impeccable innocence in their territorial imperative, generally appear ridiculous. The so-called Anglo cannot gracefully assume that the Mexican border dispute is the result of Mexican incorrigibility, nor can the Mexican carry the same concept regarding the Anglo. The old saying is that it takes two to tango. We need to establish a living condition viable for both differing cultures. Time, of course, ameliorates the differences created by old boundary disputes, though never are they fully forgotten.

But just as many Frenchmen believe that the French language must prevail in Quebec, Canada, so do many people of Spanish-Mexican extraction believe that Spanish must prevail and be spoken in the Southwest. In principle this would infer a general concept that Swedish should prevail in Minnesota, German in Wisconsin, Dutch in Pennsylvania, and so on through a vast mosaic of national provincialism based on language. Man is archetype, not of different species by country or language, and language gains no advantage when it labors provincialism and tries to become an island unto itself.

When I first arrived at my present residence in Minnesota, the local population was primarily Swedish. The large Protestant church edifice in the little nearby inland village of Scandia had only Swedish sermons, later alternate Swedish and English sermons, now only English sermons.

I have often wondered how the offspring from one French and one Anglo parent might be expected to divide their affinities in Quebec, or how offspring from Spanish and Anglo parents will divide theirs in the Southwest. Also, how should the French or Spanish capital invested in Anglo enterprises and Anglo capital invested in French or Spanish enterprises be resolved in the event of some final political dissolution based on ethnic differences.

Obviously, with universal intermarriage between peoples of different languages, the mere suggestion of language segregation becomes absurd. Succeeding generations will, no doubt, continue to stir and confound the existing polyglot mixture, until language extraction is lost in the abstraction of intermarriage. There is no language barrier where sex is concerned. When I see a professional football game and note such names on uniforms as Kelly, Garrett, etc., I assume that these are the athletic products from the so-called "Fighting Irish of Notre Dame," until later when I see them on the sidelines with their helmets removed from strong, determined, ebony black faces.

As we moved through the streets of Southwest American towns on our arrival there seven years ago, we heard quite a few young people carrying on conversations in Spanish. Many Spanish-speaking parents tenaciously holding to the tradition of their past have exerted every effort to have their children remain exclusively Spanish. The tragedy here is that these young Spanish people will someday emerge as adults and disperse in a country primarily English-speaking, where language may handicap.

The young Spanish-speaking individual might, of course, be offered an assignment, say in South America, where Spanish would be required; but, on the other hand, the number of such assignments from English-speaking countries is very limited. Where these assignments do exist, a broad comprehensive knowledge of both languages is essential.

The young of Spanish extraction should certainly continue to retain their ability to speak Spanish, but not at the sacrifice of well-spoken and well-written English—the most important communication medium they will have through life for success in an English-speaking country.

If, for a paragraph or two, I might assume the position of the devil's advocate, and even in a sense appear to contradict what I have already said about language practicability, I would like to point out that as virtual English cowbirds hatching some of our future, as it were, in a Spanish nest, I would be disappointed if the Southwest did not retain much of the indigenous, Spanish-Mexican culture. The fact is, I would prefer the lifestyle here to much of what I have seen in the Anglo-industrial rat race that pervades most of the remaining United States and Canada. But this Spanish-Mexican culture which so fascinates, we need to realize, will in a generation or two of anglicized schooling and association have become so Americanized, so industrialized, so modernized, so diluted in the flow of common commercialism, the Spanish-Mexican culture will remain in the Southwest only as a delightful, colorful, yet dimly patterned, background. I have observed that the youngsters who seven years ago carried on a merriment of play on the streets, speaking Spanish, now whoop it up in English.

Nevertheless, before the Southwest becomes too anglicized, my wife and I hope to glean from the yet-existing Spanish-Mexican-American culture, the priceless advantage that any rapidly disappearing ethnic culture holds for the edification and enjoyment of man. In the more rural area where we reside, the Hispanic culture remains more dominant than in urban areas. Thus, we may enjoy it longer by circumstance alone.

When we took up seasonal residence on the Pecos River near Puerto de Luna, it was suggested by outsiders that our position there would be incompatible with the Hispanic people who had centuries of taproots deep in the once Mexican and now New Mexican soil. So emphatically was this idea imposed on us that at times we almost felt a portent of dissent about to hover over us. If this were a calm before the storm, something in the social meteorology allowed that storm to bypass us, for little or nothing came of it. The crew we engaged to modernize our principal dwelling and put the entire premises in habitable and attractive order was comprised of both Spanish-Mexican-Americans and Anglos with, perhaps through the circumstance of predominant population, largely Spanish-Mexican-Americans.

Some of these employed refused invitations to sit at our table for lunch, preferring, it seemed, the shade of an overhanging rocky ledge or the seats of their pickup trucks to eat their own lunches. But as time went on we were convinced that this was merely a bashful phase. Eventually, as we served food and drink indoors and outdoors to whoever happened to be caught up in the reconstruction, there developed a warmth, a nonchalance—even a certain amount of friendly banter with all concerned. After seven years of seasonal residence in the Southwest, we feel integrally a part of the community.

The name, Rutstrum, though it has lost much of its original Swedish spelling, was given the Spanish inflection, "Rutstrano" by our neighbors. When I pointed out that the name, when broken up, was a combination of the words "rut" and "stream"; or, in fact, a name which might actually mean "Irrigation Ditch," it seemed to carry the indigenous quality needed for us to become part of the arid, irrigated Southwest.

The four Mexico-originated stone walls beyond the irrigation ditch became too monumental a challenge for us to resist restoration. Such restoration, we decided, would be placed strictly in the hands and under the influence of a crew of Spanish-Mexican-American craftsmen. It now provides a writing studio and alternately a guest cabin. But I am afraid that the original builders of these walls might, if they saw the modernization, toss in their sleep beneath the red Mexican soil.

No doubt, the floor of the ancient, original structure was of dirt. The *vigas,* we can assume from the soil which had fallen within, held up a dirt roof. As we excavated the interior of the walls to remove this dirt and bulldozed out a part of the mesquite in the yard, we found no trace of metal—hinges, latches or nails. When this structure was built, such luxuries apparently were not available. Some flint artifacts did turn up which, of course, were not necessarily those of the original occupants or builders. One can conjecture that the door might have hung on handcrafted wood spindles or leather hinges. The window openings had a size more the appearance of square portholes through which a defense weapon might be used against an encroaching foe. These openings we had enlarged to create windows.

What originally was the flat *viga* type of roof became, for practical reasons, a gabled one. The stone exterior was left in its original state, but I am afraid that the identity of the original walls stopped there. We wound up with varnished timbers in the ceiling; smooth, poured concrete floor enameled a warm patio orange color; white, interior, plastered walls; plank door with handwrought hinge straps, held on with rugged wrought iron lugs. The effect became massive, rugged, durable—suggesting security and permanence.

Where the original light at night might just probably have come from hand-dipped, tallow tapers, now it was flooded with several variations of electric lighting. (Why does this last fact fail utterly to excite the romance that one associates with the lighting by hand-dipped, tallow tapers?)

Did the early picturesqueness and native culture, which the original walls represented, die with the advent of refinement and modernization? I hope not. But if it did, bear in mind that the entire remodeling concept, along with the manual work from restoration of the cistern to the entire cabin proper, was, as I said, left wholly to the influence of the Spanish-Mexican-American crew. These craftsmen were given a free hand, and with the architectural and structural transition, whatever it is, from early Mexican to modern New Mexico, U.S.A., with this we happily abide.

CHAPTER ELEVEN

Water

When we saw the irrigation ditch and the Pecos River flowing gently through our property, with a cistern also filled to the brim, we remained quite oblivious to Southwest aridity. Water seemed more than abundant. Before long it was brought home to us that the Southwest pronouncement, "sky determines," was not mere rhetoric.

"Water, water, everywhere nor any drop to drink," is a well-known, sea-going quote from *The Ancient Mariner*. Its poetic tragedy evokes thought about the whole subject and problem of geographical water distribution. For the Southwest the substance of this quotation might be revised to read, "Water, water, where so rare that death hangs on the brink."

No reason, as far as I know, has apparently been given why the oceans, which cover more of the earth than land, should not have been fresh rather than salt water. Perhaps the greatest productivity on earth will come when man can economically desalt sea water, and also freshen those inland waters which are too alkaline for ready consumption by man and animal. Desalting and freshening of inland water is now, of course, being done, but to date on such a small scale it is regarded more as an experiment than substantially increasing the freshwater supply. The vast amount of fresh water that rivers empty into the salt seas would, without desalting seawater, convert the entire desert regions of the world into lush, fertile fields. Where now "forty acres to a mother cow" might seem the necessary allocation, an irrigated acre or two per mother cow from the waters of these rivers might come closer to the allocation. The fresh water that lies on Canada's Precambrian shield—in more than 100,000 lakes of substantial size in Ontario alone—is extravagantly lost in the oceans through numerous rivers, the St. Lawrence to the Atlantic, the Mackenzie to the Arctic Ocean, while numerous others flow into the semi-salt waters of Hudson Bay.

Yet, if man could so reorient the flow of this water as to irrigate all of the arid regions of the Southwest, it is a ten-to-one cinch that he would louse up the whole province of his enthusiastic endeavors, as he has so consistently done when he attempts to "improve" natural areas.

To begin with, the sunny Southwest would no longer be a civic weather boast. Evaporation would make clouds, creating extensive overcast, holding back much of the sun and greatly reducing the now clear atmosphere which is the result of low humidity. The increased high humidity in summer would make the high temperatures of the Southwest intolerable, comfort-wise—hydrologically another Florida, but hotter. The grasses which presently in the Southwest make some of the finest beef in the world would be replaced with other pasturage that would produce good milk but poor beef. The nature of the Southwest soil is such that erosion from violent torrents created by greatly increased rainfall would convert present arroyos into small grand canyons, sending billions of tons of topsoil into the ocean. Winter snowfalls would set records on both desert and mountain, with riotous spring floods. Time, I suppose, would probably make its own adjustment. At least, ground cover would eliminate the dust storms.

We need suffer no illusion or optimism on this water increase conjecture. The chances are more apt to weigh toward increased drought. Seven years ago when my wife and I first took up seasonal residence in New Mexico, we were not restricted by the amount of water we used for irrigation. Last year, meters were installed on the gates where the supply entered our irrigation ditch from the Pecos River. Irrigation water is now rationed. The per-acre allotment is ample, but as time goes on it will have to be decreased, no doubt, with successive decreases to follow.

One buys land with water rights or without them. Considerable acreage lies along the Pecos River that would make excellent farmland, easily irrigated, but the owners have no water rights. The river at this point flows generously from bank to bank, but the water needed for this deprived owner's land has been allotted downriver, and the only use it can be put to where there are no water rights is to range cattle. How these water rights have been acquired would make a prodigious volume alone, with pages stained with the blood of battles fought over the rights, of litigation that has swamped the courts, of trickery and cunning as unscrupulous as that used by con artists, of deliberate fraud run rampant through politics, bribes, and chicanery. Water control laws have been used to protect imperatives, not equities.

When it became known that we were not particularly interested in the cultivation of our tract on the Pecos, we were approached by several individuals who wanted to buy our water rights. We, of course, refused. What seemed strange was that one could have in his pocket a document that had cash value which only represented so many gallons of the water in New Mexico that could be made to flow elsewhere than where it was needed. The water we use to irrigate our land, had we sold the rights, could be used upriver or downriver, not only to irrigate a tract that by somebody's finagling had lost its water rights, but to increase the per acre feet of water on land now already enjoying ample irrigation acre footage. The purchased water rights could even be held as a document for future use as mere collateral while some landowner on the immediate flowing river suffered bankruptcy from lack of irrigation water. Water rights from upriver lands have been acquired through direct purchase, by devious manipulation and otherwise, by downriver landowners. This has created water right inequities which, it seems, can never be ameliorated unless state and federal laws are applied to the distribution of more equitable water rights. Water right equities should be an integral part of the land, not documents in somebody's pocket. Laws eventually must correct the inequities, no matter how they were created.

The uninformed might consider that water could be pumped out of the ground for irrigation and thus overcome the lost water rights. But here, too, the water is controlled. Only that which falls from the sky, and that used for domestic household purposes, is not under restrictive mandate. But even that which falls from the sky gets into occasional arbitration. Should rain be allowed to sink into the earth to maintain the underground water level, or should range land be treated with compounds or lined with polyethylene to hold the water in depressions on the surface? For watering stock, yes; for irrigation diversion, the right becomes a moot question.

At our seasonal residence on the Pecos, we have been so blessed with water, it is difficult to truly understand the other fellow's arid situation. Yet, in a way, we have become as involved. It is never clear to us when we should irrigate. A day needs to be set for the individual irrigated-land owner to use his water allotment. Our lessee irrigated when the water was up in the ditch, but complained that upriver landowners took too much water and too often left our lessee without sufficient water. We tried to solve this confusion by redigging the channeling-off ditches, installing and lowering the gates so that low water in the main ditch flowed merrily into our channeling-off ditches. But then on the rare times when the ditch was full, it roared with such fury we had to greatly curb the gate flow. When rains were minimal in the mountains, we had insufficient water for irrigation because no carefully distributed rationing of water seemed enforceable.

We are supposed to contribute a certain number of labor days to the maintenance of the community ditch. We avoid the actual labor by paying those who want to absorb this employment, and many do. We were quite perplexed when first we took up our seasonal residence, in that total strangers came to us with bills for day labor. The matter was soon cleared when we found that these paid bills for labor on some remote part of the ditch could be credited to us and applied on the annual levy made against each member of the community ditch. It seemed rather involved at first, but, on the contrary, proved to be very simple and practicable. Since employment is not too readily available by all in the Southwest, we have no trouble in meeting our obligation to contribute days of labor on the ditch by giving employment to those who wish to replace us and charge us for it.

We do, nevertheless, put in a day or two on the ditch where it passes through our property—removing the tumbleweed that continues to fill the ditch, getting exercise and soaking up sunlight. At the community ditch meetings, we humorously put in a voucher for labor and give the members a moment of levity when we donate this service to the "general welfare of ditch members."

The beneficent Federal Government has extended a low-interest, long-term loan to our community for supplying "domestic water." A generous rancher with a substantial irrigated acreage discovered in one of his canyons a high capacity spring of excellent water. Tapping deeper, it turned out to be a major water supply. Being a generous man, he contributed it as a community domestic water supply. We were invited into the membership that was set up, but the government red tape that is so traditional has not made it possible for a sufficiently equitable distribution of pipelines to provide us with this domestic water. Some members have been supplied with service while others, because of the seemingly inconsistent red tape, cannot get it. The government loan provisions require that an attorney and an engineer be hired by the membership and paid out of the government loan. How we are to evaluate the purpose of these functions I have failed to understand. If the engineer's function is to see that the pipelines are properly installed, we wonder why the pipes which carry the water are breaking over the system so badly as to seriously increase the maintenance cost. The organized membership can, at a specified time of expiration, we are told, get another government loan without having to incur the expense of an attorney and an engineer. When that times comes, costs may be so reduced that spring water can flow permanently from our taps. As the Spanish say, "mañana" (there is always tomorrow). In the meantime, we have water trucked to fill our cistern, which flows from our taps if we do not forget to replenish.

Attributes in the purchase of property are not always apparent at first. One of these was a very-much-overlooked, solid rock contour. A few hundred million years more or less of water erosion have created a small rock canyon near our dwelling, and while we have enjoyed its picturesqueness, we gave it no thought as to its possible utility as a water supply. This lack of discovery was due to the fact that we are not in residence there when the flash rains rush through the canyon in May and continue through the summer.

Weather can, however, be freaky. For the first few years, rainfall was below average. The last years an increased measure of rain has fallen

—on occasion even in the off-season. One morning we awoke to see our canyon a magnificent cataract, sending its torrential flow into the Pecos, but only after it had spilled into the community irrigating ditch, overflowing it and irrigating five acres of tilled land that as yet had no spring planting.

Where did all this water come from? I donned a rain shirt and sou'wester to explore. The shelf above our dwelling site was of solid rock. Elevations are obviously deceptive, otherwise transit level companies would go out of business. I watched the directional flow of the water. A glance at the flat-looking shelf would lead one to believe that the flow would be quite uniform and widely spill over the edge of the shelf, but gravity proclaimed otherwise. Instead, the water moved gently from all directions on the shelf toward the small, rockbound canyon, funneling it into a narrow spillway before it dropped vertically into the solid rock fissure.

The civil engineer who viewed a great waterfall and thought of its horsepower, had only a more exalted notion of what I thought, as I considered how I might, with masonry or concrete, close the outlet to that miniature canyon, and provide a substantial reservoir of water unlimited for whatever needs arose. Would the water rights to that spillway be a matter of public restriction? Since it fell on the solid rock shelf, it could not seep into the earth to raise the underground water level. If the canyon remained as it was, it could only water our own private acres, at times in such excess as possibly to be quite damaging to an existing crop. Here was a plausible reason for control.

The final conclusion?

We didn't dam it. To watch, at every flash rain, a private waterfall of our own spill majestically in an area where the name was *desert*, became too fascinating a prospect. Our aesthetic sense, as it most often has done, overruled the utilitarian opportunity. Could it be that similar decisions might apply advantageously toward the preservation of a large share of our national, natural world?

The Southwest generally receives its summer rains from massive thunderheads that move sporadically about and create destructive gully washers. The dry, sun-scorched arroyos of solid rock, and the deep caliche

The Southwest generally receives its rains from massive thunderheads.

arroyos testify to this. Sun-scorched, indeed. They seem so dry that only the wildest stretch of the imagination convinces anyone from the North that periodically great walls of water may suddenly come cascading through them. Southwest auto roads in many places pass over these arroyos, and it is not unusual to see long lines of cars, their drivers impatiently waiting out these flash floods. Now and then, the uninformed driver is caught just as a wall of water comes barreling out, the car tossed and rolled down the otherwise dry fissure, until it is no more than an unidentifiable mass of tin, glass and iron.

Perhaps the Alamogordo dam project in east-central New Mexico stands as the most cardinal example of what a Southwest flash flood can be. It was built to store the waters of the Pecos River for irrigation purposes. When the finishing touches were being put on the dam, specula-

The sun-scorched arroyos of solid rock and the deep caliche arroyos testify to the "gully washers" from the thunderheads.

tion indicated that it would take years to fill and create the fifteen-mile lake area provided for it. Work went routinely on. Then came the most fantastic news the engineers of the dam had ever heard of. Flash rains of spectacular proportions were occurring on the upper Pecos. Those who lived on irrigated tracts were piling their most necessary belongings into pickup trucks and heading for the high country. The river had gone wild. A water wall of fury carried with it the movable and the seemingly immovable. The engineers who had built and were finishing the dam saw an incredible hazard mounting. Would the dam that was built to hold back a lake created by a prolonged accumulation of water, stand this onrush that would batter the dam with an incalculable force? They doubted it. Yet it held, and what had been an estimated flow that would fill the lake reservoir in years had come pouring down in three days.

When we set about remodeling, restoring and modernizing our *adobe* dwelling, we noticed that the large kitchen floor made from six-inch tongued and grooved wood flooring had a rather pronounced arc in each board. It did not, however, affect the floor to the point where it had to be replaced. In fact, we thought the uniform shallow corrugation gave to it a pattern that was quite unique. But how could a floor warp in this fashion where the roof had been tight and the humidity that of the desert? In time we learned. The waters which had rushed through the Pecos Valley to fill Alamogordo Lake had incredibly risen to this high point, flooding the *adobe* dwelling to windowsill height. This occurred better than thirty years ago, and could, of course, happen again. But the government meteorological charts made at Tucumcari, New Mexico, suggest that this is only a remote possibility, that thousands of flash floods have come in those thirty odd years, none reaching the history-making proportions of the one which warped our kitchen floor so uniquely.

CHAPTER TWELVE

The Retirement Complex

Some years ago, to round out a book on the wilderness cabin, it was my desire to observe how people spent their time in retirement. Northerners who find with their increasing age a growing nonresistance to cold, or falsely attribute their sensitivity to age, turn their thoughts to warmer climates. Migration into the Southwest, to the South and Southeast, to Hawaii, to foreign countries with mild climates, has become a movement so extensive as to affect nearly every phase of our national life and international relations even to the point of disturbing our own gold standard and the world's currency.

When my wife and I took up seasonal residence in the Southwest we were naturally eager to visit our former friends who, having retired, had made the transition from the North to a year-round, Southwest residency. Seeing them in their new environment, facing retirement opened up some interesting aspects of man's whole sociological approach to life.

What do people do when they retire?

I asked this question of an eminent psychiatrist friend of mine.

"They die," he said bluntly.

This answer contains a share of exaggeration, of course. But it carries so much significance in the analysis of retirement, one might say that it is much too true. Perhaps elderly people die simply from being elderly, but the retirement age today is so much younger than it used to be, and the prolongation of life through medical advancement so increased, there must be more than old age contributing to the obituary notices of the retired.

Statistics do not fully tell the story, nor do particular cases. Nevertheless, both reflect on the aggregate scene, and a case or two in point may be worth mentioning. An acquaintance of mine who loved to go fishing on his vacation looked forward to the day when he could build a comfortable cabin and do nothing but fish and otherwise indulge his permanent leisure. He did retire and he did build the cabin, which is an achievement since most just talk about it. With a car, he could reach the nearest town in an hour, while in the opposite direction stretched a wilderness wonderland. The cabin modernized, and with an impressive fireplace, television, telephone, and other facilities for leisurely living, he scarcely needed more.

He fished. Days on end he fished. Then there came days when he didn't fish. In fact, there were weeks on end when he didn't fish. In time, he didn't fish at all. Another fact was that he finally didn't do much of anything. Time began to hang heavily on his hands.

A year later I found him in the city, working as a night clerk in a small family hotel. But not because he needed the income. This had been adequate, and would be. He just had to fill in the time somehow, he said.

One night as he assumed his night clerk duties, two bandits approached the desk and at gunpoint demanded the day's cash.

"Of course, boys, I don't want any trouble," he said. "Here, take the cash and go."

He opened the cash drawer with one hand, lifting the bills to center attention, while whipping out a .38 Colt revolver and firing two rapid shots with the other, mortally wounding one of the bandits, who died a few months later, seriously wounding the other, who recovered only to serve a long prison sentence.

I asked him how he reasoned his own safety with the bandits' guns pointed at him.

"I didn't give a damn if they killed me," he said. "I was a guy who was just putting in the time until the Grim Reaper arrived."

Though he was a man of compassion and regretted having had to take a life, the episode refocused his interest. People saw him as a man of great courage. The blur of monotony suddenly zoomed into a sharp image of articulate daily living. We need to be wanted, no matter for what.

I have been told that railroad conductors and engineers do not live long after retirement. I posed this as a question to a retired conductor some years ago. He merely joked about it at the time, as we had often engaged in much humorous banter whenever I rode with him before his retirement.

After his retirement, I visited him a number of times at his cabin. On my last visit I found the cabin windows boarded up. I sought to find out what had happened to him, only to learn that he had died. There, apparently, were no clear symptomatic causes for his death. He had lost weight, did not respond to treatment and finally succumbed. The theory was that he might have pulled through had he shown an interest in living.

What research I have been able to do on this subject would easily fill a volume—case histories of the retired lost in nebulous diagnosis as to why they did not survive a reasonably high average of longevity. The answer must be found in the realm of frustration, people suddenly becoming inarticulate with the industry that formerly sustained them so artificially that they could not continue to function as natural human beings.

The secret, I think, of a vital, self-sustaining interest in life can be found in watching the enthusiasm of a child. If left to his own resources, the child is scarcely ever bored. A mere pile of dirt will excite his interest. I can recall my early childhood when, having no commercial toys, I managed to float chips of wood down a rain-drenched gutter. To me, these chips were a simulation of the riverboats I had once seen plying the nearby Mississippi channel. With my voice I supplied the low-keyed rumble of the foghorns that signaled the approach of the riverboats around a bend. My chip ships drew up to tiny docks made of dirt where valuable cargo was unloaded—that is, small pebbles lined up on the ships to buoyancy capacity.

Childhood zest for life? Possibly.

But on the night of November 19, 1969, I watched the arrival of the Apollo 12 flight on the moon. Did the astronauts see a barren waste? On the contrary, they were overwhelmed and excited by the sight of a dust-filled crater and its age-old potentials.

Wherein lies the secret of maintaining a zest for living?

We have been reminded of the so-called "green benches" through the South where elderly, retired people sit, whiling away the time. One cannot say that what they lack is an opportunity for industry, because more than likely it was the repetitive, habitual, leisureless years of industry that by degenerating habit eventually put them on the green benches. Industry provided the niche and the needed livelihood, which educated the central nervous system—degenerated the nervous system is perhaps more accurate—until the individual could not find an alternative from the perpetuation and habituation of his original job. Taken away from daily industry or business, the wheels still turned idly, performing no function. They had worn grooves too deep out of which they might readily depart.

Our retired friends whom we visit in the Southwest keep telling us that we are in an enviable position when we can maintain such a high interest in life. A fair share of affluence doesn't seem to have much to do with it in their lives or ours. Wealthy playboys—and I have known a few—are terribly lonesome, often badly frustrated. I was as excited about life when I was very poor as I am now when I have no financial worries, and frankly I cannot explain it.

Frustration on retirement obviously has its greatest involvement in *habit*. Neither business, industry, nor government influence should be allowed to destroy our central nervous system to the point where we wind up on the green bench form of retirement. I could boldly suggest a three or four-day work week with two one-month vacations each year in which to offset the deterioration of mind and body by industrial habit. This, no doubt, would be regarded as industrial heresy, but it would break the habit cycle effectively enough to resolve a measure of the retirement problem. The extended vacation periods would likely be used by some vacationists for avariciously seeking extra employment to increase income. But this might be forestalled through some form of income tax penalty that would make such overtime employment futile—thus encouraging the individual to live resourcefully and more sanely, and hopefully discover how to live rather than just how to make a living.

Suggested long periods of vacation lead people to believe that the green benches would get greater occupancy since people would have nothing to do. The history of reduced employment hours and days, along with increased vacation periods, has not had this effect. Long working hours destroy the faculties for dealing with leisure as an indispensable human need. Extended vacations for the employed have grown into a multi-billion-dollar tourist business.

The puppet-on-a-string population having become this way by habituation to industry and business over a lifetime, is a much different element from those of us who by circumstance or deliberate choice have interspersed our lives with sufficient leisure to avoid hampering our central nervous system by almost-uninterrupted habit.

Since about 85 percent or better of the population now live in cities, it is obvious that the majority of those retiring and seeking the warmth of the Southwest will make the mistake of moving from cities in the North to cities in the Southwest. This, of course, is a great stroke of fortune for the approximately 15 percent of us who love and seek the kind of life in the Southwest that has the amenities of seclusion, natural environment, serenity, general health factors and escape from the horrors of increasing pollution. Even if half of the population appreciated the high virtues of natural phenomena, we obviously would have no natural environment left. Perhaps it will always be an environmentally viable world only for those of us who shun the cities and seek the natural environment. Towns of moderate size in the Southwest, earlier, held out some true advantages for the retiring element. Early Phoenix, Arizona, then with a small population, was a delightful haven for the arriving urban-minded home-seeker. But mayors were elected on their ability to encourage industry and population growth. Business fattened on it.

"Come to Phoenix and bring your sinuses with you," was the slogan.

People came, like a vast gold rush, to an ultimate overwhelming industrial population degradation. Now if you want to survive, you leave Phoenix, Los Angeles and other urban industrial pollution centers and take your sinuses, your emphysema and other bronchial damage acquired in these cities with you. The growing city: the peopled, fascinating, entertaining, luxurious city? It has become a terminally sick monster and now is dying everywhere—cue enough why we have chosen life elsewhere.

Perhaps the name of the game in metropolitan life is largely sensuality. I believe it was Norman Cousins who said, "I understand the higher mathematics but I can't handle it."

There is nothing wrong with sensual pleasure if you can handle it. A man, digging in a ditch for eight hours can handle a frequent big thick steak or its equivalent with all the trimmings—benefiting by it. Too often, of course, he can't afford it. The same dietary program will kill for certainty, long before the average life span, the individual who lives the commonly practiced sedentary life of the retired. Those who have retired from industry or business and live in metropolitan centers become compulsive eaters because they find little else to do. And since the eternal cocktail generally points up the luxurious meal, and makes less boring the passive life, liquor soon also becomes the between-meal anodyne to thwart the monotony, with frequent, consequent alcoholism, or at least, obesity.

Could all of this have been different? The question which arises upon such speculation is whether urbanism did not become a form of orientation, which at first seemed creditable, but in the final "development" evolved into a kind of psychosis—a degeneration. At one time we considered urbanism as the earmark of civilization. It was antipolar to the primitive. In fact, we even regarded the farmer as far removed from the refinement, the suavity, polish and so forth of the urban-developed citizen. Materials and modernization of urban life also flowed to suburbia and eventually to the farmer. Distinction between rural and urban culture faded. Suburbia in its earlier phases had managed to capture the better part of urbanity and had incorporated in it some of the natural values, which gave the suburban residency an advantage even for the urban-minded resident.

But megalopolis has destroyed suburbia in the big sprawl. Greater fragmentation of land parcels and the locating of vast shopping centers within the megalopolitan spread has destroyed the advantages by urbanization of earlier suburbia. The retiring Northerner entering the Southwest has incidentally become the victim of this real estate concept. If he finds sufficient acreage to give him elbow room and a natural environment, he is either burdened by the resulting excessive real estate taxes or he is farther away in miles from what he has been accustomed to or wants to be.

The gregariousness developed from urban habitation is such that few are capable of sustaining themselves in a remote region. The canary, though he was once a free and magnificent creature in the Carpathian Mountains, if turned loose from his cage to his original environment would flounder and soon perish. As we have too often seen, the lifetime-urbanized citizen becomes awkward to the point of being constantly accident-prone or suffers a coronary when suddenly subjected to the more vigorous activities of a natural environment. We can suppose from this that on retirement he largely needs to remain in his urbanized cage, in his home or car, and keep his perspective limited to city walls, for most have lost by decades of urban subjection the physical capacity to cope with a natural environment, and too often have lost the faculty for enjoying the immensity, the grandeur, the fascinating complexity and profound nature of it all. It takes a lot of natural exposure and know-how to grasp its values—a condition most overurbanized citizens would deny. If man is, as a recent book portrays him, *the naked ape,* he has by this very hirsute inadequacy been largely compelled to cage himself for survival. A few of us have seen the need to "grow a little hair" and revert to freedom.

Those of us who have lived for a great time in a naturalistic environment are amused, if not perplexed, by the assumption that urban life is the normal state and that removal from the urban grind is paradoxical in principle. With most of the people living in cities, this general misconception, of course, should be understandable. *Herd* and *maverick* have their own connotation.

When my wife and I sought a seasonal residence in the Southwest, we thus bypassed 85 percent of the human Southwest habitat. We were looking for a natural environment residence which six out of seven would not seek. Or, adversely, our six-to-one advantage in finding what we wanted made competition, fortunately, minimal, though other factors, as I have stated elsewhere, made a discrimination in physical site selection somewhat of an environmental problem.

Choosing a residence in a naturalistic environment has seemed to some of our urban-bound friends as merely a manifestation of the primitive in man that "civilization should cure." Here, again, civilization has been confused with urbanization. *Man the animal* is a phrase that is avoided in any discussion of urbanized man. The biggest industry in the country is that which concerns the cosmetic struggle to hide the animal-structured creature that is man. He does well as animal, being a rather wholesome and magnificent creature when living in a natural environment. Within the walls of his strictured clothing, within the walls of his home, which in turn is within the walls of the city, he physiologically becomes the world's greatest problem, one that seems destined to destroy him by pollution with more certainty than a potentially looming nuclear disaster.

The essential biological process of elimination seems in the urban environment to be man's greatest curse. Underarm perspiration alone has set up a billion-dollar business, wherein he seeks to block a form of elimination for purposes of fastidiousness at great risk to his health. The poisons which have to be eliminated under the arms now are blocked by cosmetics to accumulate and poison the whole system. One might go on with the numerous other artificial efforts of man to hide himself as basically animal with consequent health risks, but the subject is not a pleasant one and I am sure the reader is largely aware of what they are. TV commercials at mealtime obtrude their offense all too blatantly. In short, man has not succeeded in obscuring his animal nature through the conventional curtain of artificiality. Could he not live closer to a natural environment conducive to his animal nature and be a more genuinely civilized creature in the process? If not wisdom in man's adaptation to a more conducive environment, what is civilization? Must it be ecological despair?

The biological nature of the *Man Animal* is obviously such that he cannot any longer tenably live in the industrially artificial complexity of the big city and survive with optimum physical and mental health, or even hygienic or sanitary decency. This by now should have become so academic, the least rationalization ought to suffice in rescuing the astute individual at least from prolonged urban exposure. It will not, of course, rescue the masses. We have come to regard the city in terms of convenience. Few ever stop to regard the meaning and effects of convenience.

Industry has set its course on it. The effect has been that convenience has resulted in a dangerously passive life, not an indispensable, physically-active one.

The problem confounds itself. Clinical statistics show that when women washed their clothes on a washboard, coronaries per capita were much more limited. The convenience of the automatic washer and dryer of clothes keeps women fat who, as a result of obesity, develop coronaries. Well, what do you do about it? There isn't much you can do about it unless you can set up an alternative for exercise. We could reason that to overcome many of the coronaries, we should go back to the washboard, but, of course, this becomes absurd. Restoration of the washboard is absurd, but the principle involved is not, because women who live passive lives pay a dear penalty for it. Golf, the urbanized man's concept of exercise, isn't of much value, though a very minimal move in the right direction. Reducing exercise must be vigorous enough that one freely perspires. This, to most, seems too uncomfortable a prospect, though the first initial exercise soon dispels this feeling.

A passive life reaches out for diversion from monotony. Alcohol and tobacco have become statutorily permissive crutches on which monotony can lean. They are fallaciously thought to be a means of escape from tensions, though the aftereffect only compounds such tensions, adding to the original boredom. A careful check has shown that people who retire to cities somehow eat, drink and smoke more than those who pursue a more natural and physically-active life. Sensual habits seem to be pursued as a diversion from sedentary discomfort.

Marijuana will likely be included before very long in the established permissive list of the escape-by-dope products. Penalties for possession are rapidly being reduced. The argument has been that it is no worse than alcohol or common cigarettes, and it is believed that marijuana will provide another means of escape from boredom.

Man does have an alternative choice. The difficulty lies in the fact that adequate perception of a better life is hard to come by from a bad, or wholly foreign, vantage point. Habit and fortuitous circumstance have most of us by the scruff of the neck. The individual making an unconventional choice is inclined to be regarded only as unruly. The exploratory urge is strong in some individuals, but generally it seems to be weakly endowed.

The human being, I believe, is so constituted that to the degree he as an enterprising individual is able to involve himself in natural phenomena, and to the degree that he can dispense with extraneous artificiality, will he glean from life those profound values which contribute most to his enjoyment. He will likely not discover the validity of this until he makes the first few overtures toward change. It becomes not a matter of *moderation in all things,* a phrase which I find offensive, but more a matter of intellectual discretion.

If I were to point up one salient factor in my own life that has more than ordinary significance to me in the always vague pursuit of happiness, it is that the cherished values available to me now when my means are more than ample, are the same values which were available to me in my earlier financially meager years. The more natural approach to life simply transcends much of the gadgetry and industrial junk that clutters up life. A high degree of material selectivity keeps the storage spaces of life open for the reception and retention of greater values.

CHAPTER THIRTEEN

A Few Flies in the Ointment

One of the conversational games we sometimes play when well-traveled friends gather at our fireside is: "Of all the places on the North American continent that you have visited, where would you rather spend the greatest share of your remaining lifetime?" The answers are so varied and the qualification of the selected places so novel, it is not difficult to see why the world as a whole is everywhere-populated.

To presume that some region in the world comes closer to environmental perfection than any other, as considered in Chapter Nine, involves so many naturalistic factors, personal viewpoints, so much anthropology and ethnic consideration, one could only append the perfection concept with, "perfect for whom?" The hurricanes that run the alphabetical gamut of women's names in the southeastern United States, would, to some people, make life there too hazardous. The "twisters" that periodically level whole towns in Kansas and adjoining states are to others as frightful. The fear of earthquakes has prevented a share of migration into California. Almost perpetual winter rain in various parts of the Pacific Northwest discourages those who prefer more sun. Just as many people fear the Northern winter. And so go the natural deterrents everywhere. The artificial deterrents that prevent a choice loom up as large.

Our casual examination of the documented world's land areas showed only two places as having a year-round uniform temperature—one in southwestern Australia, the other on the Ethiopian Plateau. I do not recall what the problem was in Ethiopia, but in southwestern Australia, apparently all seems ideal except the water. That is too offensively brackish. And we haven't overlooked the fact that a uniform, comfortable temperature the year round could be most degenerating.

We, just as other Northerners on arrival in the Southwest, have found the 85 percent sunlight highly conducive to the enjoyment of living. But sunlight here entails a problem—aridity. "This would be an ideal country," said one Northerner, "if there were normal rainfall."

And, of course, what he is suggesting is that aridity has its problems —the dust storms.

You take the good with the bad, I reasoned, especially where the good predominates. A working philosophy, no doubt. It presumes a fundamental need for light and shade, a balance of contrasts in the processes that make up human existence. This philosophical formula, however, just didn't work where I have tried to reason down a Southwest dust storm.

For over a half century I have met the elements of wilderness travel as I found them over various parts of the continent; temperatures that dropped below 50 degrees Fahrenheit in Canada while mushing a dog team down a river, so that I had to get into camp to avoid the temperature hazards for both myself and the dogs. One fall while I was on a canoe trip, it rained for twenty-nine days straight, the temperature just high enough above freezing most of the time to prevent conversion to snow—perhaps the worst of all weather. Other times blizzards have come when the day before the temperature had been a plus 50, dropping so fast that one either battled the fury or went into camp for a three-day hibernation.

This was adversity, of course, but weather is also a phase out of which adventure in a wilderness is made. It is natural, elemental, understandable, and somehow made tolerable. One can provide for it with acquired competence, even boast of one's ability to meet the challenge better than others do. But Southwest dust storms are not natural; they are outside the compass of wilderness competence. They are the result of man's gross stupidity riding on greed. In order to glean every dollar from the range, man has grazed the land down to the roots. He has ripped open the ground with a plow to attempt cultivating crops on arid land fit only for grazing where the sparse grass crop should have remained to hold the soil and retain the low moisture content. Man's ravage of nature and his lack of ecological sense have been a sad commentary on his whole boasted civilization. He just hasn't learned that the soil needs moisture retention by growth cover and that he cannot possibly graze beyond a minimal moisture retention level. He looks to the sky for moisture when a large share of it has to be in what might metaphorically be termed, "vegetation clouds." He believes that the forests of the Southwest should be cut down "because they absorb too much moisture." When he tried this in some areas, the soil washed away from rapid run-off, and blew away from lack of moisture-retaining undergrowth.

What is a dust storm like?

Dust storms can come most any time, but are most frequent in early spring. Assume that you are not out on the wilderness trail, but ensconced in a modern, supposedly tight dwelling, whether countryside or town. You have been looking forward to one of those numerous, delightful Southwest days. All seems conducive to another day in the sun. The wind begins to rise, not excessively at first, but within an hour it is of gale proportions. Your view an hour ago extended to the far mesas. Now it does not exceed fifty feet, or in towns, even across the street. The slight clearance under the doors, that wouldn't permit access to most insects, is now ample for a build-up of sastrugi-like ridges of finely ground red sand across the floor. Around windows it sifts in, driven under pressure by the wind. It drives up under the roof and spreads in a thick layer across the attic floor. It gets into door locks until your keys fail to work.

When I think of camping out in the Southwest, the focus is largely in the mountains where increased moisture minimizes greatly the onslaught of dust storms. But the interest is not always in the mountains. To pack a horse and set out for a camp on the desert can be an enriching and profound experience. It can also be an abominable venture if caught in a dust and sand storm. Much of this, I suppose, comes under the heading of fastidiousness. I once knew a lady who loved flower gardens, culling and weeding without stint, but she had some peculiar aversion to grit and could not handle soil with her bare hands. This seems carrying an aversion rather far, but I can sympathize with those who cannot tolerate sand in their eyes, nose, mouth or elsewhere, and in all forms of equipment. In the lava areas of northwest New Mexico, the sandstorms can grind the windshield of a car until it looks like a piece of frosted glass and the paint on the car looks as though it had been sandblasted, which it has.

Recent better rainfall cycles have improved the dust storm situation considerably for us in our area, by bringing up weed coverage growth. We arrived in New Mexico after several years of subnormal rainfall, and presumed that this diminishing rainfall would continue, or even grow worse. Naturally, we are elated over the increased rainfall, but abnormally high rainfall cannot be expected in the desert, especially where man has extended himself to destroy by overgrazing the moisture-retaining properties of ground cover, causing rapid runoff rather than high evaporation. The dry cycles will, no doubt, come again as they have in the past. Few of us are overly happy about excessive government interference with private endeavor. Yet, the need to compel ranchers to limit the number of cattle they can graze on their acres is as imperative in a sensible ecological process, as there is a need to prevent natural ravage in any other respect.

We manage to transcend the sand and dust storms by knowing there are long intervals of calm, when on waking we reiterate being glad to be in the Southwest and alive. We have sealed all possible dust ingress around our door and window openings of our *adobe*, sealed off the attic, and put sponge rubber gaskets on tool boxes and instrument cases. There has to be some sort of solution to man's problems. We persist in finding the solution to our own.

Another fly in the ointment is our feeling of concern for the Southwest Indian. Earlier in Southwest history he was in a native position to give battle where incursion upon his lands and rights reached intolerable proportions. As I have mentioned elsewhere, he took a toll of his white invaders unparalleled in military strategy and can at least recall with sadistic delight his revenge upon his persecutors. But today he has little advantage against the forces of an adverse society that would denigrate his position rather than ennoble it.

While much of the land which the Indian managed to retain did not have the grazing qualities of areas usurped by the incursive white element, nevertheless, it did have some grazing value, though with his population increase, is now economically stifling. The reservations earlier were extensive enough to make livelihood adequate. Since then the Indian population has grown as it has everywhere. He is outbreeding the whites at a higher ratio. It is no longer possible for his entire population to be confined on the original reservations. For a hundred thousand or more Indians to glean a livelihood from an allocation of land sufficient for only a fraction of this population is brewing up a storm in the Southwest as deleterious as the dust storms.

The wisdom of early reservation tribe leaders was to make the reservations the communal property of all Southwest Indians concerned. To allocate communally-owned tracts to individuals as has been proposed by shortsighted politicians catering to special elements and make it possible for the Indians to sell their tracts, would soon leave the Indians of the Southwest with no land at all if my knowledge of land sharks has not been shunted. Indians have not been able to hold their own in the highly competitive industrial and land procurement madness that has swept the Southwest as well as the rest of the country.

With Indians unavoidably spilling over reservation boundaries, this ruse is now being employed by legislators to provide for individual ownership of reservation lands. Obviously, the ulterior motive here is to swallow up the reservations in white man's commercialism.

What despair of the Indian I see in the Southwest bothers me because I am always hoping for some measure of my own personal serenity wherever I live. I cannot, therefore, without feeling like a scoundrel, live on an island of isolated affluence while children on life's mainland cry themselves to sleep from hunger. When the sun casts its glow upon the river mesas, I would enjoy this spectacle a lot more if I knew that a good supper was being prepared in every Indian's cabin, that his evening under the desert stars would be as serene as mine, that he would look upon me as warmly as I look upon him, now with both warmth and compassion—in the future, I hope, with warmth and no need for pity.

Another fly, which to many may be regarded as a mere gnat, is the corruption of native culture, largely practiced in the curio shops. The Southwest had its hand on the solution to much of its Indian problem when it first featured the products of Southwest Indians. Pottery, rugs and silver jewelry made by Indians were possessions that the tourist gladly opened his pocketbook to acquire. Such products could have developed to

Genuine Indian pottery—or the product of common industry?

a point where the Indian needed no assistance whatever. The handmade silver trinkets, the fascinating pottery and the Navajo rugs could have become so intimately associated with the Southwest, and specific other Indian regions, a worldwide demand for these products at profitable prices would have raised the whole economical level of the Indian and put the Southwest, especially, in a position of high tourist distinction.

What happened to those priceless Indian pieces?

Corruption.

When you enter a curio shop in the Southwest today you will find the most devious language in the sales talks. Or, silence allows the buyer to assume that the pottery, silver jewelry, Navajo rugs and other items are Indian products. There are genuine Indian products to be had, but no legislation enters into the picture to show that most of what you see piled high and wide in curio shops is the shoddy turned out in factories over the country and abroad. A large portion of the silver jewelry and trinkets, which the tourist presumes to be made by Indian metal craftsmen, is but the punch-press stampings of some factory. Much of the gaudily decorated factory pottery and the imitation factory "Navajo rugs" comes under the same fraudulent category.

The Southwest is not alone guilty of this corruption. It is manifest just about everywhere, but this is a book on the Southwest. Also, the Southwest stands out more saliently in this respect because it has a vast, extraordinary Indian culture that is being used fictitiously to back up the factory fabrications.

An effort has been made legislatively to require that a label be put on the items, but lobbyists and political subsidizers manage quite well to continue the fraud of pretending that the factory-made shoddy as marketed is Indian craftsmanship. Perhaps the most insidious of the practices is the consigning of stock to Indians, to carry out the pretense that the factory items were made by the Indians selling them.

It would take time for the Southwest to purge itself of this menace, but I believe that in time it could be done to a great advantage in rebuilding the Southwest Indian culture and making the Indian economically self-sustaining, to say nothing of dignifying the Southwest curio shops. All items that suggest Indian manufacture ought to be labeled exactly what they are. Misrepresentation should be subject to fine. Some factories would, no doubt, employ an Indian or two to continue the fraud, but it is up to the Indian and his departments to stop such perfidious practice.

Just as great quantities of factory-produced pottery, silver trinkets and Navajo rugs are palmed off as genuine, so are a share of arrowheads. Here the problem is much more difficult. Not so long ago the knapping of arrowheads was thought to be a lost art. Now arrowheads are being produced commercially of such close imitation, it is difficult to distinguish them from the pristine product. Just as Indian pottery, a great painting, or a true sculpture can be genuine, so should be an arrowhead. Actually, it is the tourist who presumes false items to be genuine, the salesman making no claim. The Southwest has an unlimited amount of flint rock lying just about everywhere on the surface and in the desert soil, from which the commercial arrowheads are made. Curio shops also have a substantial supply of arrowheads molded from plastic, flint-colored glass and other materials. One can understand the molding of plastic arrowheads to simulate such rare arrowheads as the Folsom head where the only purpose is to reveal the design, but the commercial pretense is too often misleading.

Tourism is, no doubt, one of the Southwest's most valuable resources. Strong organizational forces need to emphasize and protect its most cherished values. Climate is one of these natural resources that attract the tourist. But the tourist cannot be sustained on temperature alone, even though he is well fed, well housed and charmed by scenery. There is something basic in the Southwest Indian culture that needs a strong guardian defense, if it is not to diminish and be made a tourist farce. Such monuments and villages as Canyon De Chelly, Montezuma Castle, Tonto, Navajo, Tuzigoot, Casa Grande, Wupatki, Hopi in Arizona, Chaco, Acoma and others in New Mexico point up the basic Indian culture treasure the Southwest can hold for the tourist. While a share of these monuments and villages are now mere ghost ruins, much is known about them from artifacts and other means. The descendants from the people who once lived in these places may be hard or impossible to trace, so that there can be no Indian-made craft items for the tourist. Yet, there are artifacts from the culture of the early people, and these can be simulated. No matter where they are made, if such items are carefully labeled as simulations, no problem should arise. Merely to flood the market with factory-made items and label them as Indian pottery, which most of them do not in the least resemble, is to bastardize, and to destroy the Southwest's greatest asset.

If I might be allowed to pluck just one more fly from the Southwest ointment, it would be that of discouraging the movement to run asphalt into and around the monuments so that the tourist can phlegmatically view them from the seat of his car. The foot trails to parking areas need not be so long but what cars can be kept well away from the monuments.

The same might be applied to natural camping areas. Where trailers need asphalt, one can understand the imposing of roads, but should not foot trails and horse trails lead to inviolate areas beyond the asphalt? Must the appeal be made for only those who come roaring in with their cars, asking "Where is the biffy and the Coke machine?" to the exclusion and desecration of the Southwest's most priceless values?

CHAPTER FOURTEEN

The More Natural Approach

Perhaps the most elusive factors concerning man's existence are those pursuits conducive to his happiness. The search for happiness can, of course, be like the search for truth. Both upon critical analysis become hopelessly involved. Any formula for what might contribute to man's happiness must obviously beg the question—happiness for whom? Despite this individualistic consideration we cannot escape the general fact that man deviates little anywhere from his prototype—a species of animal with basic elemental needs: fresh air, fresh water, balanced nourishment, and vigorous exercise in the open if he is to sustain optimum physical health and a lust for life. How these basic needs, so pertinent to his physical welfare, affect his mental processes has been the subject of much speculation. The idea that fattening of the body can mean fattening of the brain, is expressed facetiously, of course. But the clinical suggestion that deterioration of the body by overeating, smoking, smog, alcohol, lack of exercise, and other physical debilitators can lead to brain deterioration does not seem farfetched. The victimized are naturally compelled by their perversions and addiction to be willful thinkers, but when half of our hospital beds are occupied by mental cases, we can assume that something artificially disastrous is at work disrupting the natural and wholesome process of life in general. If these seem largely academic matters familiar to all, we might ask, what does anybody do about it for himself?

We need suffer few illusions on this score. Where 85 percent of our population have packed themselves into cities, the individual's chances of becoming detached from his place as an integral cog in the machine and seeking a full and healthful existence is minimal in our society as a whole. While this is tragic for the masses in an overpopulated world, it is great fortune for the minority who seek a healthful, serene and humanistically tenable environment.

This individualistic choice of urban escape does not imply isolation or social aloofness. While my wife and I have sought to remove ourselves from urban centers in order to breathe, relax, and find healthful diversion, we do on occasion brave the traffic canyons, smog, sound and fury of the city to enjoy the benefits of art galleries, the symphonic hall, theater, libraries, and friends—retreating as soon as possible from our urban cultural predations and social obtrusions to mull over in the quiet of the countryside whatever cultural loot and warmth of humanity we have acquired.

It may seem a bit presumptuous, but I believe the enjoyment of these cultural and social advantages by our intermittent attendance allows a higher degree of assimilation when removed from immediate convenience than when they can be had around the urban corner. And this basic concept, I think, applies as well to the choice we have made where residence does not become too indigenously confined to the remote countryside. One tends to become more aware of country life's intrinsic values when not permanently tied to the country scene by occuption. There is, of course, no happy balance of this kind in the life of the individual who is confined fifty weeks to industry and allowed only two weeks of pleasurable rehabilitation in a natural environment. It figuratively suggests too much the "fifty-fifty stew, one cow and one rabbit."

It is not, of course, only the urban victim of industrialism who becomes involved with the imbalance in material, natural and humanistic values. To treat the natural environment in the same strictly utilitarian sense as that of urban industry, where the materially productive returns of the soil become the chief focus, is to limit life's advantages just as drastically. There is, however, less chance of this in the Spanish-Mexican-American culture of the Southwest than elsewhere on the continent. The term *mañana,* mentioned earlier, quite clearly explains why this is so. We have friends who have small businesses in town and small ranch areas in the Pecos Valley. Just how profitable dollar-wise these ranch areas are,

I have not been able to determine. I would be more inclined to believe that they are utilized primarily for the diversion needed in life than anything else, which is one of the most fruitful crops that man can harvest. When these people reach the valley they seem in no special hurry. A long, leisurely coffee break with us requires no special arm-twisting.

There are others, of course, who have ranches in the valley, businesses in town, and special commitments elsewhere. They labor as though there were no tomorrow, and were compelled to buy their way into the beyond. Also, there are so-called "sportsmen" who come into the valley primarily to glean from their sojourn, meat pounds. But one must not overlook in this group the fellow who carries a gun under his arm for conventional reasons which he scarcely ever fires. Popularly, there seems to be a kind of illegitimacy in a pleasure jaunt through a natural region unless it can be qualified on some materially profitable grounds.

As to our seeming provincialism, of which we are on occasion accused, seasonal residence in four entirely different environments tends to make us, I think, less inclined to develop provincial habits. The closer we live with what we believe to be the emending processes of nature, the more we become products of our environment, of course. But just as we have avoided being conditioned wholly by the neon lights of the metropolitan pose, so do we avoid being wholly conditioned by one particular natural environment.

Ecology briefly is the total interrelationship between organisms and their environment. This, of course, suggests a very significant relationship of man to his environment—but more than biological. The effect of natural beauty, for example, on man is also something that has to be considered in his development. The question arises whether man can get along without this natural aesthetic effect and maintain his fullest equilibrium as an optimum psychologically sound human being. His instinctive desire and need for natural rather than artificial beauty are perhaps not too well understood, even by psychologists who generally concern themselves least with nature. It may be that natural beauty is an absolute essential to man's welfare, and one of the reasons why urban society is deteriorating by an ecological imbalance.

We are gradually beginning to understand what happens to man when he breaks this ecological chain. It has been well depicted in a series of TV specials, "Ecology, The Final Crisis." We have, obviously, not reached a high enough civilization to enter upon the study of what we could call, The Aesthetic Ecology—man's absolute need in his finest development to feed his mind with natural beauty. If man does not eventually eliminate himself in toto from the earth by his reluctance to recognize ecology as organisms relating to the preservation of his environment and his physical self, then perhaps he might gradually discover the psychological effect and need of natural beauty in his development as a whole human being.

Perhaps few of us are as consigned to nature as my wife who after spending some time in Alaska, suffered a kind of nostalgia because she craved the sight of a glacier. I have awakened in the morning in a hotel and felt the grim austerity of looking out of a window and seeing only the bleak utilitarian walls of buildings across the street, with a feeling of depression—no breath of fresh morning air, no song of nature to inspire.

Morning usually breaks clear and extravagantly beautiful over the Pecos. Reaction to natural beauty is, of course, varied from being to being. Personally, I get a strong feeling of wanting to share it with others, say with some work-weary miner who will spend the day underground, or a Harlem youngster playing in his smog-ridden asphalt environment.

Whenever I am caught up in the grandeur of sunrise over the desert, or the spectacle of desert bloom after the spring rains, I become aware of individual man's greatest poverty—*time*. If this time factor could be pointed out with certitude (but, of course, it can't) perhaps there would be less passion for greed, less self-imposed servitude in industry, less friction between man and man, less racism, more leisure to enjoy the precious moments of life that are rapidly ticking away.

While considering beauty and its effect upon us, perhaps that composite spectacle of bloom on the Southwest desert should be given a classification among the categorically established seven wonders of the world. I can't think of anything, unless it is the autumnal coloring of the Northern hardwoods, that outdoes it in grandeur. "The miracle of growth"— trite may sound the phrase, but never dull the actuality in the desert. To have a full compass of the desert bloom, we need to arrive upon the scene after the winter drought and just before the spring rains. The earth then looks sterile and incapable of giving forth any significant growth. When the rains come, usually in May—suddenly there is an aesthetic explosive bloom. From out of the apparently sterile ground shoot up astounding, vast varieties of multicolored flowers that bring only "ohs" and "ahs" from the most taciturn.

A woman of our acquaintance in the North expects a telephone call from us when and if there is an unusual year of bloom. She boards a plane and travels two thousand miles merely to stroll for a day or two through the floral grandeur. "The next time you come," I said, "bring some underprivileged woman with you, one who has only a single geranium plant blooming on her tenement windowsill."

Today we are amateur botanists; tomorrow, amateur mammologists; next week, perhaps amateur archaeologists—amateurs ad infinitum. What we learn about the Southwest from one seasonal visit to the next could not contribute anything significant, I am sure, to the sum total of natural history. Yet, one can afford to consider the lay population—that overwhelming majority who have neither time for scientific understanding, nor interest in it—those who know little about the natural environment in which they live but derive pleasure from a casual interest. To some of these people we can perhaps bring a little light. I was asked by the civic head in a nearby prosperous town how I liked our new residence down there on the Pecos. The conversation ran something like this:

"It's an intensely interesting region," I said.

"How do you mean?"

"The Pecos River Valley and the surrounding desert area are a great wilderness wonderland."

"In what way?"

We went to the nearest coffee shop so that I could explain what a greenhorn in the Southwest could possibly find in the Southwest removed from the multiple lures of a city. I thought he was "pulling my leg" when he invited me to give a talk to a businessman's luncheon on the natural phenomena of the region.

"Frankly," he said, "I didn't know very much of what you have told me about the Pecos and I am sure that most of the luncheon guests would not be any better informed."

While I did not, of course, accept his invitation and presume to talk about the natural phenomena of the Southwest desert, I was generally aware of his indictment. In this hurry-scurry world, scarcely do you find those who can answer your simplest questions about their immediate natural environment. A tree might grow in Brooklyn and all who see it possibly derive enjoyment from it, but few would likely know what kind of tree it is, nor why a tree is important to life.

If we recognize, not disparagingly, but reflectively, that we are mammals—primates that walk upright and have the advantage of using artificial means to carry on life—it seems easier to make an adjustment to this natural environment on the Pecos and derive happiness, than attempt an adjustment of the mammal to a wholly artificial urban area.

Man survives after a fashion within the compass of his urban artificiality, it is true. The difficulty is that he must function incompatibly there—not as a natural, physical creature but more as an urban mechanism.

Plagued by his animalism where he is out of his environment in urban artificiality, man has been compelled to hide it the best way he can in the "refinements" of industrialization.

The reminder of this animalism as incompatible with his urban environment is constantly brought into the living room by the medium of radio and television. As we consume our food from delicate china, set formally on linens, amid candelabra and sterling silver, we are served TV courses on bad breath neutralizers, corn plasters, deodorants, sprays for reducing nasal and sinus mucous, dandruff deterrents, laxatives, hemorrhoid applications, psoriasis remedies, and as many more to remind us that urbanized we are not the creature benefiting by exposure to the physically ameliorating effects of sunlight and fresh air. We are not as the wildfowl, beautiful in a natural environment, not as the magnificent mustang on the open range; but rather we are as the chicken, the cow and the hog, cooped, stabled or stied with our physical offenses.

Beyond the routine of optimum physical adjustment, what about man's *cultural* ascendancy over the basic mammal that he is? Or perhaps we should ask more particularly, under what sort of an environment can man achieve his greatest intellectual or humanistic approach to life? We might assume by the way our industrial strife is going that humanism is the most neglected phase of man's hope for a valid claim to a dignified civilization.

There was a time when cities were small, tensions moderate, and the environment fairly conducive to healthful living. Gradually, as cities grew and became environmentally intolerable, we observed those concerned with humanistic affairs moving to the outskirts. Literary and artistic production in England, for example, became almost synonymous with the floral-bedded cottage at the countryside. Thus, the humanistic approach surely must suggest diversion from the noise and fury of mechanization, the intolerable pollution, if it is to flourish.

Selecting a seasonal residence based on a humanistic approach to life, we can scarcely avoid choosing a natural environment where it is possible to carry it out: humanism, as defined by Webster's Dictionary, being "an attitude or way of life centered on human interests or values, a philosophy that asserts the dignity and worth of man and his capacity for self-realization . . ." As an urban resident for a number of years, try as I might, it seemed impossible to equate this definition of life with an environment where man is a captive of industrial smokestacks and office building walls.

In a copy of the New Mexico magazine I note that one of its late governors was doing everything in his power to encourage industry to come into New Mexico. It seems strange beyond reason, in the face of the nation's worst problem—irreparable pollution of air, water and soil—that he wants to destroy the magnificently natural state of New Mexico as soon as possible, substituting its valuable and never-failing resource of recreational tourism with a forest of black-spouting smokestacks.

Lincoln said, "If you can't plow through a stump, plow around it." Similarly, cultivation of body and mind has for us seemed far more rewarding by the urban bypass. If the reader should assume that such a life means isolation, he might consider the popular expression, "Do your thing."

For, if you do it well, or your best, someone will find you no matter where you are. And we must say that surely some have—and to our delight—

HAIL GUEST!!

"We Ask Not What Thou Art

If Friend . . . We Welcome Thee With

Hand & Heart

If Stranger . . . Such No

Longer Be

If Foe, Our Love Will

Conquer Thee."

Quoted from a classic of old? No. Though teetotalers ourselves, we copied this from an old gin bottle.